E. Templar

out!
in
the
name
of
Jesus

out!
in the name of Jesus

PAT BROOKS

Creation House
Carol Stream, Illinois

©1972 by Creation House. All rights reserved
Printed in the United States of America
Published by Creation House, 499 Gundersen Drive, Carol Stream, Ill. 60187

New Leaf Library edition
First printing (June 1975) 10,000

First printing (December 1972) 10,000 copies
Second printing (October 1973) 5,000 copies

International Standard Book Number 0-88419-105-2
Library of Congress Catalog Card Number 72-94834

This book is dedicated to
the Lord Jesus Christ,
Who is the
Deliverer

"He that dwelleth in the secret place of the most High shall abide under the shadow of the Almighty. I will say of the Lord, He is my refuge and my fortress: my God; in Him will I trust.

"Surely he shall deliver thee from the snare of the fowler, and from the noisome pestilence."

Psalm 91:1–3, *King James Bible*

Creation House
Carol Stream, Illinois

CONTENTS

Acknowledgments

I praise God for His mighty help in putting my life together. In addition, I wish to thank the many human helpers He used, without whom I would not have been able to share through this book what God has done.

First, Don Basham, pastor and Bible teacher, and Bob Walker, editor of Christian Life Magazine, for their excellent counsel and encouragement.

Next, my dear friends Eleanore Smith and Beverly Strott who helped me, not only with typing the manuscript, but by reminding me of crucial details from experiences when we ministered together.

Next, Eleanore Smith again and her husband, Carl, for an extremely thorough job proofreading the manuscript. Other friends who proofread sections of the manuscript were my aunt Maude Williamson, Hope Traver, Millie Nunez and Elsie Bohlander.

Finally, the precious people whose testimonies are given in this book. In some cases their identities have been slightly disguised (although not in all) and other names have been used. However, the accounts of their defeats or victories—the truth of their experience with the Lord and battles with the forces of darkness—have been kept intact. Surely it is their prayer as it is mine that sharing these testimonies will result in a host of people coming under the love and lordship of Jesus Christ and overcoming Satan in His name.

Quotations are taken from the NEW AMERICAN STANDARD BIBLE by permission of Lockman Foundation, LaHabra, California.

1
Snare in Suburbia

Suburbia, U.S.A. Cornerstone of the American dream. Citadel of family life, motherhood, and right living. Garrison of respectability, civic pride, and the faith of our fathers. World of well-kept lawns and freshly black-topped driveways. Scene of summer barbecues and winter meals by candlelight. Land of big company transfers and upward mobility.

Suburbia, U.S.A. Façade of the American establishment. Hospital for divorce, abortion, and debauchery. Prison of scandal, hypocrisy, and Sunday morning religion. Cosmos of ill-kempt emotions and eroded morality. Stage of cocktail parties and lone drinks before breakfast. Sea of unrest, selfish ambition and economic insecurity.

It all depends on the point of view.

Julie's hands shook a little as she started to clear the last few things from the dinner table. She was glad to have something to do and even gladder that the dimmer switch on the chandelier was turned all the way down. Looking first at the bowl of floating camellias in the center of the table and then at her own trembling hands, Julie decided not to chance an equilibrium test. The table cloth could stay on until tomorrow morning.

Hal was still charming her mother with those old navy stories of his. Mrs. Delbert sat gazing into his soft brown eyes, chuckling every few minutes as he delighted her with one tale after another. This had been going on for nearly five and a half hours—before, during, and after dinner. Somehow Julie had stumbled through the meal, said the right things at the right times, and gotten the children off to bed; but dragging out the evening like this made the situation impossible. Hal was getting more and more reckless in the things he said as the evening wore on; furthermore, he was just drunk enough to say something that could ruin their whole lives.

As she came back from the kitchen, Julie motioned to Hal, nodding toward the front door. She pantomined her request from the doorway, standing behind her mother. Hal was across the table from Mrs. Delbert, grinning broadly. His only move after Julie's suggestion in charades was to rock back in his chair with his arms folded on his chest.

How aggravating of him, Julie thought. *Why, he has no intention of leaving any time soon. It's so obvious.*

"Well, I've already stayed up long past my bedtime," Mrs. Delbert was saying, wiping her eyes. "I don't know when I've laughed so much or had more fun. This has been one evening I'll never forget."

"It has been great fun, Mother," Julie said as casually as she could, "but you are right. It's late now, and I think we all need to call it quits for one day. After all, Hal, Mother just got here from Arizona yesterday. We've been keeping her going every minute since she came. She's not used to so much excitement and such long hours."

"Well, the evening is still young as far as I'm concerned," Hal said, sprawling further back in his chair and putting his hands behind his head. "Julie, I'm getting dry. I think we need another martini."

"Don't you think we've had enough to drink tonight, Hal?" Julie asked, her eyes pleading with him as she spoke.

"No, I don't," he said, winking at her nonchalantly and jumping to his feet. "I'm going to make us each one more drink. How about that?"

"None for me, Hal," Mrs. Delbert said. "I really am going to bed now. Thanks for coming over. Julie, you're fortunate to have such a wonderful next-door neighbor. I'm sure he keeps your family entertained."

Mrs. Delbert went up to her daughter, put her arms around her neck, and gave her a warm hug.

"I'm pretty proud of you," she whispered. Then in a normal voice, "Good night, folks. See you in the morning, Julie. Just wake me after you get the children off to school, and we'll have a leisurely breakfast. Okay?"

"That sounds wonderful, Mother. Get a good night's sleep now. We'll be up fairly late tomorrow night too, because Roger's getting in from his business trip on a late afternoon plane. He'll want to sit up and talk to you."

Julie waited, frozen, in the dining area until her mother's bedroom door had completely closed behind her. As she clenched her fists three or four times, she could feel her sweaty palms. Cold, clammy sensations went all through her body. She had never been more afraid.

"Hal," she said softly, "listen to me. You've got to go home right now. This has been one terrific evening. I don't think you have any concept of what I've been through tonight. You can't stay here any longer. Is that clear?"

"You don't really want me to go, Julie," Hal said as he walked up close behind her, slipping his arm around her waist and giving her a drink with the other hand.

"I've already told you I don't want another drink," she said, her voice breaking. "I just want you to go home. I want to get this night over with and try to get some sleep. It's been awful."

Julie fought to hold back the tears as she pushed Hal away and walked into the living room. He laughed as she took the first two sips of the drink. This made her furious; she felt like such an inconsistent fool. She slammed the martini down on the table next to the wing chair.

Hal walked over to the couch, put his drink on the coffee table, and threw himself back against the pillows. He had propped them up earlier in the evening as he relaxed there before supper. It had been his tacit way of saying, You may as well invite me to stay for dinner, because I have no intention of going home.

He folded his brawny arms on his chest and began to talk in an easy, comfortable tone of voice.

"You know, Julie, your mother likes me even better than you do."

"Oh, how could she help but like you?" Julie said in complete exasperation. "Everyone likes you. You can be a dream when you want to be, but you sure weren't a dream tonight. The whole business was a nightmare."

Hal looked over at her, his eyes taking in her soft, strawberry blonde hair that fell casually on her shoulders and bobbed provocatively when she tossed her head in emphasis of her point. Then his suggestive glance dropped slowly to her neck, down her pink gingham dress, lingering briefly on her slender, shapely legs.

"You look gorgeous in that dress," he said huskily. "You're all woman, Julie, and you and I both know it."

"Hal, this is no time to talk like this," Julie said, whispering now. "You must keep your voice lower. Mother is right on the other side of that bedroom door. There is no place in a ranch house like this where we are free to talk while she's here. Don't you understand?"

Hal shifted his hands back behind his head and looked up toward the ceiling.

"You know, Julie, when Charlie spotted us in the back of the restaurant last week, he couldn't take his eyes off you. Boy, he sure was jealous, and I enjoyed every minute of it."

"Hal, won't you leave now, please, for my sake?" Julie pleaded with him as sweetly as she could. "If we make a false move now, everything we've shared together this past year is in jeopardy. Don't you see that if you keep on like you did tonight, we're going to be found out?"

"Found out by whom?" Hal asked, narrowing his eyes into

grim slits as he looked back at her—an expression she had only seen in him once or twice before when, like tonight, he had been drinking heavily. "Your husband doesn't appreciate you. In fact Roger is the biggest jerk I know. He doesn't deserve you. He never did. Sometimes it really burns me up that you have to keep on living with him until things straighten out a little better financially, and you and I can be in a position to do something about our own lives."

"That isn't the issue right now, Hal," Julie said. "What I'm worried about right now is tonight's fiasco. Why on earth did you make that remark about helping Tony last week with his airplane model until about eleven o'clock and then going home at three A.M.? You put me in a ridiculous position, forcing me to make up that stupid story about throwing a blanket over you on the couch because you had fallen asleep. Can't you see this is no good, Hal?"

He chuckled easily as he settled back into the pillows.

"Why not, Julie? It's just like your mother said. I enjoyed every minute of the evening. I wouldn't have missed it for the world."

"Well, I could have missed it," she said in a barely audible, savage whisper. "I stand to lose a great deal more than you do, Hal, and I think that's why you are just thoughtless about times like this. You've got to remember, I have my three children to think of. With your wife away in a mental hospital and no children, it doesn't really matter to you if everything should break wide open. Your life wouldn't change that much, but I'm trying to keep this home together for the sake of the children. Lately that's been bothering me quite a bit."

Julie got up from the wing chair and began pacing up and down the living room floor, biting her lip and stealing a quick glance at Hal. There he lay, sandy hair tousled over his tanned forehead while he watched her intently. Suddenly, without any warning, he shoved the coffee table as far as he could, well down past the end of the couch, and with one more quick lurch pulled Julie down on top of him with the same arm, while reaching up with his other hand to turn out the light on the table behind his head. In that one fleeting instant before the room went dark, Julie saw something in Hal's eyes that she had never seen before. All the warmth and compassion which had drawn her to him in the first place were gone; in their place was naked lust. She froze in his arms, afraid to resist. Suppose some telltale noise should rouse her mother or the children? For a moment the only sound in the room was Julie's wildly pounding heart.

"No, Hal," she finally whispered, "not here in the living room with everyone just a few feet away."

"Yes, right here, *now*,". Hal rasped back at her, his words forcing his will upon her like steel nails being driven into a rotten, decayed board. "You don't dare make a sound, or your mother might open that door."

Later, as the front door closed behind Hal, Julie picked up her clothes—her shoes, girdle, and stockings—and slipped into her room. The pain in her chest was terrible. It was like something she went through every time she had intercourse with Roger, her husband. She always hated every minute of that.

To think that she had been used like this by Hal! It was so grotesque, so unlike anything they had ever experienced in their intimate times before. Julie's hands went up to her head as she threw herself down on the bed with a low moan, sobbing convulsively. All the anguish and guilt of the evening poured in upon her in one terrible moment, plus the awful irony of her mother's last thoughts of her "dear, sweet daughter."

Suddenly her life began to flash back before her eyes as she writhed in revulsion at the unwelcome panorama in her mind. *This must be what it's like to drown,* Julie thought. *I've heard of people going through something like this when they're drowning.*

She could see herself back in college days falling in love with Bob, then running away from him because he couldn't consider marriage yet and she was already engaged to Roger. She could remember those awful four or five months near Roger and his family before the wedding. They were so critical; nothing she could do was ever right. Being with Roger was hard, for she had no special feeling for him. What weird sense of duty made her go through with the wedding anyway?

Oh, how her head pounded as she thought of the wedding. She let out a low moan with the memory of the effort to act the part expected of her as a happy bride; how devastated she had felt inside. No one knew or understood her.

Then the honeymoon—oh yes, the honeymoon. Could she ever forget Roger's elaborate attempts to make certain she enjoyed their physical relationship as much as he did? He had read all the books, knew all about the timing, the places of sensitivity, and the rest of it. But did he know anything about her thoughts; her need for someone to understand her? She had tried to have the right feelings to go along with it all, but he had been so harsh.

At first she had put it down to inexperience and new, hungry passion. However, he stayed that way over the years; his sex appetite and inept approach remained the same. Every night, no matter how tired she was, no matter how she felt, she could depend on it: whenever Roger was at home, he always wanted sex.

Then there were those lonely years when the children were small. Roger was always money hungry. He never seemed to think there was enough security in what they had, even though he was an accountant with a good job. He refused to go out with Julie socially but spent many long evenings working on people's tax returns to make extra income.

About that time she had discovered muscatel wine. It was cheap—about a dollar for a gallon in those days. Just a small wineglass did wonders for her attitude toward Roger when he came home at night—for a while. In a few months the wineglass became an eight-ounce tumbler. By the end of a year it took two or three tumblers before supper to give the same lift.

She had learned to refill the old gallon jug from the new

one to keep Roger from finding out how much she was drinking. She gave a twisted, bitter smile into her pillow as she realized how clever she had been in keeping Roger from knowing the truth. He had no idea she was an alcoholic.

Julie could still shudder at the thought of their tenth anniversary. Suddenly she had come to a place of resignation and had made a decision in her mind: *If we can't make a go of this and both of us are going to continue to suffer, then I'm going to end it.* It was odd that Hal should have moved next door to them so soon after that.

Hal noticed little things about her like the way she was always reading, and he would bring her the new best sellers. Oh, how she loved those paperbacks from the drug store. They took her away from the life she really lived for hours at a time. These were the days of *Forever Amber, Sex in the Suburbs, Peyton Place,* and many others. She had read them all. Gradually the whole idea of trying to be true to a husband she didn't love seemed ridiculous.

Once Hal walked into her life, there were long-stemmed roses and surprise phone calls. To him she had a face of chiseled beauty and a figure Venus herself would envy. He noticed every dimple, every half smile; so she began to smile again. He understood. They could talk together, sometimes for two or three hours on the phone, while Roger was out working on tax returns.

In the late afternoons, he would drop in to tell her some hilarious story or help the children with their homework. He would listen to them as they told him their problems—something their father was too busy to do. The children loved him.

A vivid picture of a motel room crossed her mind. Why, it was the one she had stayed in with Roger on their vacation trip to New Orleans. This "second honeymoon" had been engineered by her mother shortly after the death of her father. Mrs. Delbert sensed Julie and Roger were having difficulties, and offered to stay with the children so they could get away. Julie had looked forward to a little gaiety and to being with people. She laughed in bitterness as she remembered the way it really was. Instead of taking her out to special places, Roger insisted they spend every evening in the motel. She felt used, morning and night, like a prostitute. How she hated him by the time they came home! What a relief it was to get rid of him even for overnight, while he drove her mother back home.

Soon after Roger and Mrs. Delbert had left, Hal had come to the back door. With that winning, loving smile of his, he seemed to understand. Neither of them spoke; Julie just flew into his arms. Although they had never even kissed before, it seemed right to be his, particularly so in contrast to the wrongness of that whole miserable week with Roger.

That afternoon marked the beginning of their affair. The physical relationship with Hal had never been painful; in fact, it brought her real happiness. For the first time in her life, Julie felt like a real person. She mattered to someone. She was important. When Hal was there with the children, she felt they were a *family*.

But it hadn't all been rosy. Suddenly the merciless mirror in her mind reflected the day she stole into Hal's house when she couldn't get him to answer the phone or the door bell. Julie caught her breath in the same short, staccato way she had that day as she had entered his room and found him unconscious on his bed. He had been dead drunk. How hard it was to get him into the shower and sobered up enough to get off to work! It must have been caused by the pressure of his love for her and the hopelessness of their situation. Surely he was no ordinary drunk. Not Hal.

Another time she couldn't rouse him and had to call his doctor. Clammy fear returned as she remembered her weeks of worry afterward. Had she ever met that doctor anywhere? Would he recognize her voice? She agonized over whether he ever tried to find out who made the call; after all, Hal's wife was in an institution.

Well, what if Hal did drink too much? His behavior tonight was the result of that and the awful pressures on them. Someday things might work out, then neither one would *need* to drink so much. Without the brandy she kept hidden in the bathroom, how could she endure the awful pain in her chest and back following intercourse with Roger? Surely she was entitled to some relief. What else was there?

Tonight had just been a bad dream, that was all. In his great love for her, Hal had forgotten himself. The drink had made the strain of her nearness too much for him. Surely she still had her dream-come-true.

A shaft of moonlight crossed Julie's tormented face from a narrow opening in the draw drapes at the nearby window. Just a suggestion of light in the deep darkness, but a beginning. Were these doubts now stalking her mind letting in some unwelcome light too? Would her dream romance end, "not with a bang, but a whimper?"

Three weeks had gone by, and mother was now back home in Arizona.

The grandfather clock in the living room gave two somber gongs. Roger's steady breathing told Julie he was finally asleep. She tiptoed into the bathroom in her bare feet, closing the door before she turned on the light.

The linen closet was just inside the door, on the right. Julie reached for the brandy bottle which she kept on the top shelf under the sheets. It was about three-fourths empty. Her stomach turned in revulsion at the thought of Roger's lovemaking of just an hour ago. Life was unbearable. She held the bottle up to her lips and drained its contents.

No, she thought, *I just cannot stand sex with him any more. I'm not going to go on with this farce.*

Suddenly the brandy bottle slipped from her shaky hands. As it fell into the sink the neck of the bottle hit the faucet, and a large chip broke off. Julie looked at the chip, just about the size of a nickel, then picked it up with her right hand and began to work it back and forth across her left wrist.

Soon the red flow began. Enchanted for a moment by the trickle, she stopped and watched it spill into the sink. Then realizing she would be getting weaker before long, she took the fragment of glass in her left hand and began to cut her right wrist.

In no time there was blood all over the sink. She turned on the water and watched the red flow become a muted pink before it swirled down the drain.

Suddenly a sickish fear swept over her. *What will it be like to die?* she thought. *Why did I ever do this anyway? Why should the fellow who caused me all this misery lie in there while I go through this? Let him come in here and find me. It'll be good for him! I hope the sight haunts him for the rest of his life.*

She picked up the brandy bottle and threw it against the closed door, screaming in a mixture of rage and fear as she did so. Miraculously, the bottle bounced against the wood without breaking and fell on the bathroom rug.

Julie did not have long to wait for a reaction from the other room. In a few moments, the door was yanked open, and a very wild-eyed Roger took the situation in at a glance.

"Why, you crazy nut! What on earth have you done?" he asked Julie, grabbing her elbows roughly and looking angrily from her jeering, defiant face down to the bleeding wrists. Then he spotted the brandy bottle on the floor, and he dropped his arms to his sides. Slowly he leaned down and picked it up, lifting his face to stare at her in a strange mixture of disgust and pity as he straightened up.

"Why, Julie," he said softly through clenched teeth, "you're a lousy drunk. That's what you are. I've been kidding myself for a long time about this. I've been a fool; I can see that. How many other other places in the house do you keep these? How much money do you spend on this little habit of yours?" His voice had begun to rise.

"Shut up, you fool!" she hissed at him in a whisper. "You'll wake up the children. I'd—I'd rather not have them see me like this. They can see the body later when the mortician has dressed it all up to look pretty."

"You're not going to die, you idiot!" he said, opening the medicine cabinet roughly and getting out the box of gauze squares and the adhesive tape. "You sit down here on top of the toilet seat and let me dress those wounds right away.

The very idea of your doing something like this right when I'm being considered for a big promotion with the company. Can you think what it might mean to my career if they find out I'm married to an unstable, suicidal drunk?"

Roger sat his dazed wife down, putting a towel under the bleeding wrists which now lay passively on her lap. He worked feverishly to press the cuts together under the gauze bandages and then tape them up tightly to hold them that way.

"There," he said finally, heaving a sigh of great relief as he looked down at his work. "You're going to be all right now. What ever made you pull a trick like this, Julie? What got into you?"

Twelve years of no communication between them reduced his question to mere rhetoric.

"I don't know," she said vaguely. "I don't know what made me do it."

Strange eyes looked up at him out of deep sockets above dark circles. She was starting to feel sleepy. *He can clean up the mess in here himself,* she thought. *I'm going to bed.*

The next morning a forlorn figure stood at the edge of a sand lot, her hands shoved deep into the pockets of her windbreaker. Julie was a strangely incongruous, isolated presence in a crowd of enthusiastic parents watching the Little League baseball game.

Tony was pitching, and she just had to be there. Roger was off working on a special project for his company; he was confident that success in the thing would put him in line for the biggest promotion he had ever had. Julie tried to keep a fixed smile on her face in case Tony should look at her. After all, she wanted him to know somebody loved him and cared about his game.

Every few moments Julie took her hands out of her pockets, tugging nervously at the long sleeves of the jacket. She could feel the bandages just above the buttons.

Slowly Julie's eyes searched the faces of the adults standing near her absorbed in the game. *No one seems to know I am here at all*, she thought. *Maybe I don't even exist. No, that can't be true. The pain in my chest and back and the soreness of these cuts are real, very real. Maybe I'm invisible. Yes, that must be it. I'm invisible and nobody can see me.*

As she looked into the eyes looking beyond her out to the ball field, Julie wondered: *Is there anybody else here as desperate as I am? Is there any answer for me?*

2
Snare of the Drug Culture

Twelve years passed. The days of Little League games were gone forever for Tony. He and his buddy Ken were in the big league now. As servicemen in Berlin, they had tasted the heady wine of escape from home and family restraints. They had drunk deep of the kicks—and of the dregs—of the youth subculture.

Ten days ago they had become civilians, and were now traveling across Europe together. It was a beautiful June day in Puttgarten as the two boys waited on the dock for the late afternoon ferry to Denmark.

Tony still wore a khaki shirt, but there was little of the military about him in the white maxi-length trench coat, black handlebar mustache, ill-kempt, straggly hair, and sloppy ten-day-old beard. His furtive, darting beady eyes gave him the look of a suspicious character. He had played the part of one of the heaviest dopers in his company to the hilt.

Ken, on the other hand, who dropped acid about as often as Tony and started the days stoned on Black Afghanistan or Red Leb (hashish), was deceptively innocent looking. His expressive blue eyes gave his youngish, handsome face an appealing sensitivity enhanced by the new beard. The only trace of army left in his dress was his field jacket underneath which he wore black cords and a black and white horizontally striped mock turtleneck sweater.

After they boarded the ferry, the two fellows took their packs off their backs and stored them in racks on the main deck; then they went up on the empty rear sun deck. It was a good place to smoke.

As the whole ship shuddered under the combined impact of the engines and the low, sustained roar of the departing whistle, the young men dropped into deck chairs near the rail. Tony had the papers and the grass; he rolled eight joints in about five minutes. Swarthy and moody, he looked more the typical world traveler than Ken, who got carelessly jovial on pot. After a few minutes of smoking, both boys got up and stretched; then they leaned over the rail and watched the water.

It was a sparkling, crisp day. Beneath a cloudless, Dresden blue sky, the sea was a satin carpet, serene and shimmering. The effect was of settled peace.

"It's great to be *free*," Ken said, thinking that no duty rushed him back now. "This is a good environment for dropping acid."

"Well, there it is," Tony said, slipping a small, folded piece of cigaret foil out of his pocket. He fingered two Yellow Sunshine tablets from underneath the foil flaps, popping one into his mouth and shoving the other at Ken.

Tony pulled out two folded chaises from the wall of the cabin, and both of them stretched out to enjoy the lazy sunshine. Mellow on tea, they had about a forty minute wait for the LSD to come on; so they smoked a couple more *j*'s and rapped.

Less than an hour after they left Puttgarten, the acid trip was on. First Ken noticed the familiar churning—the butterflies in the stomach, while the rest of his body quivered slightly from time to time. His mouth seemed filled with sawdust; he worked his tongue around in a vain effort to moisten it. Occasionally he jerked his head from side to side like a possessive squirrel with a highly prized acorn.

Gazing up at the bright blue sky, Ken noticed a flock of sea gulls gliding overhead. *That's a good subject to get involved with on this trip,* he thought. For the next two hours he stared at them as he got into his mind. The gulls flew in majestic, serene gliding motions just above the wake of the ship. Never once in all that time did Ken see them flap their wings.

Suddenly Ken's whole mind burned with one absorbing thought: *Why are those gulls up there?* He looked over at Tony, who appeared to be gazing at them too.

"Tony," he said, "why do you really think those sea gulls are there?"

Tony looked over at Ken, startled. He did not answer.

"Have you noticed," Ken went on, "they seem to have a flying pattern?"

"Look at that baby sea gull. He's not in formation, is he?"

"He's trying to be," Ken said. "There's warmth there. He *wants* to be with them. Could there be a supreme being behind all this?"

Again Tony looked startled. He fidgeted nervously in his seat for a minute or two; then he got up and went below.

In less than ten minutes, Tony came back. His head was shifting from side to side like a frightened rat. Occasionally he looked backward over his shoulder to see if anyone were following him.

Ken laughed. He was beginning to feel restless too; so he decided to take a walk. It was a good idea to change his environment now anyway. He didn't want his mind to get any further out. He went below.

As Ken opened the door to the enclosed room on the main deck, he felt as if everyone were staring at him. Hostile eyes, conveying faint amusement at his tripping, made him recoil inside. He felt out of place, weird, inappropriate. Suddenly he turned around, retraced his steps through the door and hustled up the back steps to the safe, lonely sun deck again.

Wow, Ken thought. *This trip is heavy.*

Before long the ferry jolted to a stop. Ken and Tony could hear the commotion of the disembarking passengers down below, but they did not make a move. How long they sat there neither one knew, but eventually a Danish voice barked up the steps. Evidently they were being asked to leave.

Somehow Ken and Tony managed to shuffle downstairs, swerving from side to side as they joined the few people still in line at the customs counter. After everyone else had gone through, Tony went right through. Ken felt nervous and afraid. He wondered who the fellow in costume was, standing with his arms folded and obviously waiting for him.

"Come on over, Ken," Tony wailed, as if calling to someone off in the distance, although they were just twenty feet apart. "Come on over. You gotta go through."

Ken stumbled up to the counter. He shoved his passport at the customs official without looking him in the eye.

"How much money are you carrying?" the crisp, official voice said.

Ken got out his traveler's checks and handed them over. Suddenly, in his daze, something seemed very wrong.

"Hey, Tony," Ken shouted. "He wants my money!"

Wordlessly the customs official handed back the checks with great disgust. *Obviously on drugs,* he thought. Shrugging his shoulders, he let Ken through.

As the two ex-GI's made their unsteady way from the dock of the small Danish town, it was almost dark. The gray of the late dusk was an oddly fitting backdrop for the confused condition of the two young men.

"Let's get out of here," Ken said, walking with Tony toward a country road leading out of town.

They hiked about a quarter of a mile in complete silence, Tony a few feet in front of Ken. Every step took great effort. Finally they sat down on their packs, still making no attempt to communicate with one another. Ken sat with his chin on his hands, elbows propped on his knees, and looked over at Tony.

About twenty feet away the swarthy youth was flipping through the pages of a comic book, his right hand held out in accepted hitch-hiker style although there was no traffic in either direction.

The sight of his buddy in this condition gave Ken a funny, queasy feeling. *Wow! His mind is completely blown,* Ken thought. *He's really freaked out.*

As it got darker and darker, Ken felt more insecure than he ever had. He seemed to be slipping, slipping, slipping —although he was still seated on his pack. No one knew or cared about him here. Who would do anything if he freaked all the way out?

Just at this point in Ken's thoughts, two young teenage girls came up to Tony and offered him a piece of candy. Tony took it nonchalantly, not offering to strike up a conversation.

That's nice, Ken thought. *That was a good thing to do.*

Then the girls walked over to Ken, handing him a piece of candy as they continued down the road toward home. Ken's eyes followed them, dwelling on their departing legs.

Why not follow them? he thought. *They're kind of cute, and it might be a place to spend the night.*

Suddenly Ken jumped up off his pack and ran over to his buddy.

"All right, Tony," he said belligerently. "What was wrong with that?"

"Nothing," Tony said, shrugging his shoulders. "If you wanted to go with them, that's your business."

Ken's head was reeling as he walked back to get his pack and strapped it on. *How come he knows what I'm thinking, and I know what he's thinking? All the times we've gone tripping, we've never been this freaked out.*

By now it was quite dark and a high wind was blowing. There was no shelter where the boys had stopped; so they made their way down the road to a gas station, not talking at all as they walked. They took their packs off and laid them next to the wall of the building. Ken got out the tent and tried to put it together, but it was no use. His coordination was so hampered that he could not get the pegs into the holes. He slumped down on top of the tent in despair.

"Tony?" he asked finally. "Why are we going to Copenhagen?"

"Well, Ken," the reassuring voice came back, "we're civilians now, and we're on vacation."

"Okay, Tony," Ken answered a little less fearfully. "That's right."

"Hey, wait a minute," Tony snapped back at him in an altogether different tone of voice, "you know that's not *really* why!"

The harsh, cruel quality in Tony's remark was like a poisoned arrow piercing Ken's brain. Suddenly Ken felt like thick, oozing molasses was seeping through his cerebrum. His head hurt terribly, and he started to cry.

The wild, bleak night with its eerie shadows and shrill wind blended together with Ken's consciousness of mental slipping. Soon he felt himself being dragged down, down, down. Icy, unreasoning fear gripped his heart and he kept his eyes closed for several minutes. When he opened them, he felt that he was trapped in a pit, yet able to see outside it. Far down the road he saw neon lights spelling out the words Good Time Inn. In terror he realized that he could not get at good times any more; his whole body pulsated with a *condemned forever* kind of consciousness. The sign seemed to say to him that he had missed it in life, and there would be no further chance for him.

"Tony," he yelled out in terror, "we're in hell."

"I know," Tony said with a sombre finality Ken had never heard before.

He desperately wanted Tony to disagree with him. Now there was truly no hope at all. Ken's sobs became louder and more uncontrollable. He fell to his knees and fumbled with the tent pegs again. He couldn't even touch the pegs to the holes, much less fit them in.

"Tony," he blubbered, "I'm going to make the tent. We're going to crawl in there and go to sleep. In the morning something is going to be different."

There was no answer from Tony, who was now standing up and looking down at him. As Ken looked up and saw the strange figure, in the long trench coat and huge mustache, silhouetted by the gas station lights, an awful thought crossed his mind.

He's the devil. I'm in hell, and he's the reason for it. I want to kill him. If I put the knife in him, he'll just blow up like a puff of smoke. Then I'll be out of hell and back on earth.

Ken reached for his switchblade in his left front pocket. He kept opening and closing the knife. Somehow he just couldn't do it.

All right, if I can't kill him, he thought, *I'll just have to kill myself. I've already missed it; so I may as well end it.*

He tried to stab himself in the chest, but the knife only nicked the field jacket. His arms felt like water; he had no strength to try again. He threw himself onto the ground face down, his arms and legs sprawled out in four directions. Then he pulled his arms over his head. By now his brain felt like bolts of lightning were striking it from all angles. Each electric shock brought a compulsive thought with it.

If Tony's the devil, why couldn't I kill him? Why couldn't I rid the earth of that menace? Why is there evil? Why couldn't I kill myself? If I'm in hell, why can't I kill Tony? Why can't I end it all and kill myself?

A whirring sound in Ken's head seemed to blend all the questions into one great, siren-like *why* echoing down some corridor in his mind. Each new thought was a little *why* rudely interrupting the grand, noisy *Why*. Soon all the *why*'s fused together and echoed back and forth.

Why? Why? Why?

3
Fantasy, My Youthful Climate

Ken is not the only one who has ever asked why.

As a little girl growing up in the Shenandoah Valley, I often used to wonder why there was a world at all, and why I was here in it. Wandering up the hillside where we lived, I liked to lie for long hours in the tall grass, looking up into the clear Virginia sky. Sometimes I felt like I could reach out and touch God. I longed to know Him. If I spoke right out to Him, I'd imagine He was answering me when the wind blew softly. A gentle breeze came to symbolize to me His whispers to my soul.

Scripture was scanty in my home and church experience. The most I knew of Jesus was what I gleaned from a Bible story book I had, pocketsize, profuse with illustrations and sparse with words. Two pictures in it made me cry: one that pictured Him as the good Shepherd carrying home his wayward lamb, and another of Him nailed and bleeding on the cross, beneath some heavy clouds. I used to wonder why men did that to Him, or why He ever let them do it.

I loved to read, and feverishly stuffed my active mind in

a kind of mental gluttony. There was a strange, empty place inside, never satisfied in all my search. Now it strikes me as odd that no one ever suggested I read the Bible. Instead I went the way of the brothers Grimm and Hans Christian Andersen.

For a while, I got hooked on fairy tales. Gradually the idea came to me that life's fulfillment would involve getting swept up into the arms of my knight in shining armor, who would lift me off the mundane earth and take me to his never-never land of happy-ever-after. Little did I know that such delusions were concocted in the brew of European witchcraft, often considerably toned down in American versions of these tales. However, this reading bred in me an appetite for fantasy much as television violence and shows like "Dark Shadows" do for children today.

These were the years of Shirley Temple movies, Saturday morning "Let's Pretend" radio shows, and the dream romance operettas of Jeanette McDonald and Nelson Eddy. "One Day My Prince Will Come" became a kind of theme song in my thinking. Once I met him, everything would be all right.

Nights held many terrors for my imaginative mind in those early years however. Once or twice I thought I saw a blob of white in the corner of my room, but I was too frightened to cry for my parents to see whether it was real or not. Always I listened for noises when the house was dark. In fascinated horror I would close my eyelids tight, with teeth and hands clenched, conjuring up morbid notions of savage attacks upon me or my family. I lived in dread of intruders creeping up the stairs or lurking beneath windows, but I had a grit-your-teeth-and-bear-the-darkness philosophy and did not turn on the light.

My father worked for the government, and we moved about every two years until we settled on Long Island when I was a teenager. It was hard to be the new girl so often, left on the outside for months while others had friends they had known for years. I spent a lot of time daydreaming in these new situations.

Gradually I developed a yearning for marriage to a man who would be the very center of my existence. I could see myself fetching slippers for this modern knight in best nineteenth century fashion and sitting on the hearth at his feet.

When I was fifteen I met a handsome, sensitive flyer who had just returned from the war after suffering severe head injuries. He had wavy, blue black hair and deep, expressive eyes, which met mine in love before a word was exchanged between us. He was gentle and kind, a deep thinker with a pensive wisdom which captured my mind as surely as his love won my heart. He was the embodiment of all my childhood dreams and girlish longings, and fitted perfectly into every secret tableau of my thoughts. He brought into my life an explosive power of new affection, which alchemizes ordinary circumstance into a golden moment.

One night we sat on the shore of Little Neck Bay, near my home on Long Island. The moon had slipped behind a cloud, and there was no shimmering pathway of light to brighten the dark waters. I had just known him for a few weeks. Slowly, very deliberately, he turned my face toward his and looked into my eyes.

"Did you notice what just happened?" he asked quietly. "The light is gone."

"But that's because there are clouds tonight. The moon will soon be back." Why did my heart pound as I said these words?

"No, it will not come back, not for us. The clouds are there, and nothing you or I can do will ever drive them away."

"Why? What clouds? What do you mean?" I knew his moods and sensed he had picked this way to tell me something.

"Every night in recent weeks, I've had the same dream, Pat. I'm flying very high, on some kind of mission, when suddenly the bomb bay door falls open. Down I go—down into the clouds."

I reached for his face with both my hands. "Then I'll be there to catch you and hold you. Put me in that dream."

Suddenly his eyes were misty, his face etched with tragic resignation.

"I've tried, believe me, to put you there. But it won't work. This way I go alone, soon. Some months ago when I was in New Orleans I went to a fortune teller, and she confirmed my worst fears. I have very little time left, and I cannot let your life be ruined by centering it on me."

"But why believe her? Why believe those dreams?" The words were wrenched from me in searing pain, in a voice I scarcely recognized as my own.

"Because of this," he said, pointing to his head, "because it's true. Forget me, Pat. You have a full life stretching out in front of you."

"Without you?" I whispered.

He nodded wordlessly and in a few brief moments had walked out of my life.

Months later I heard of his final illness and brain surgery. His family discouraged visitors because his final suffering and confusion was so pitiful, but I found him in the hospital and saw him once before he died. He did not know me. Waves of shock and grief poured over me. I was only sixteen years old.

At his graveside I felt just as dead as he. Oh yes, I could breathe and walk and talk, but inside a light had gone out. Something in me had died which plunged my soul into a winter wilderness. My heart was mummified in sadness. It was as if some strange, dark power had crept into my life and taken away my power to love.

The dreary days of aching grief stretched into months. I began to wonder what the future could possibly hold. Someone gave me a ouija board. My mother had a friend who could "make it work," and she and I would sit together, our hands on the odd little table, as the planchette whisked around the board, spelling out answers to our questions.

It never occurred to me to wonder why it moved or to question the source of this strange power. However, soon after the ouija board playing, I began to have weird experiences at night. An ominous presence seemed to approach me, breathing in a sinister way right next to my ear in a different rhythm from my own. Terrified, I would call out for my parents. They would turn on the lights in my room and try to reassure me. I never got up the nerve to tell them what I heard, for I knew they might think I was having auditory hallucinations. Once, when I saw a sudden roomful of hideous diabolical faces, they did take me to a psychiatrist. She said these were a projection of my grief and assured me that someday my loss would be made up to me.

"Why, someday," the doctor said with a winning smile, "you will meet someone who will not only be like the one you lost; it will be he! You may have to wait until you're thirty-five or so, but you'll get together. Just wait and see."

She didn't seem to think I needed further counseling, so I never saw her again. In a few weeks the nocturnal breathing ceased, but then my health failed. I began to suffer from dizzy spells, anemia, and severe low blood pressure. More than once these functional disorders nearly put an end to my school career.

After a year or so, I learned to laugh again, but it was only the holiday decoration for a winter landscape blanketed in ice and snow. Relationships were frothy. No one I dated held my interest more than a few weeks. Although I could put on a show of surface gaiety, my life was muddled by a disturbing inner darkness. Invisible chains kept me from really enjoying anyone or anything. Like a frozen lake, my personality was dormant, waiting for spring.

Restlessness and tension were the earmarks of those years. College agnosticism produced a spiritual wasteland in me, and I often thought, *Where is God?* Still, in the lowest depths of this darkness in my soul, I knew He must be somewhere. *Was it possible to find Him?*

At graduation I looked back on the four college years with bewildered disgust. Motivation had been lacking, study erratic, dating disappointing, and my health frail. I had had a couple of near brushes with marriage, and about the only sense of satisfaction I knew was that I had managed to escape them.

Senior week I was supposed to go to most of the functions with a friend from Harvard. Actually, I gave him the tickets to Tufts night at the Boston Pops, so he could take another girl while I frolicked all over Boston with a married professional man. He was fascinated with me, and we were planning to take a trip to Bermuda together, where I imagined that I would learn to be immoral in the most romantic setting possible. However, even after I had lied to my parents, telling them I was going to visit an ex-roomate on the Cape, Brad called and cancelled out. I can still remember that kind voice.

"It's no go, Pat, I just cannot do it."

"Why not? Do you think your wife will find out?"

"No, that's not the problem. I just don't want it on my conscience, that's all. I know you've never had an affair before, and I'm not going be to the one to mess up your life."

"Why not? It may as well be you as someone else I like less. You and I get along just great!"

"Yup, we do, which is probably one reason I'm finding it impossible to play the cad. Go home and be a good girl, and I'll phone you the next time I get down to New York."

I was annoyed and disappointed at the time, but over the years I have thanked God for that man who could be unselfish and act the gentleman when I had no desire to do the right thing. His marriage evidently deteriorated after that even more, because I did hear from him when he came to New York and saw him once the following year. He had not forgotten me. In fact, he wanted me to consider marrying him. He would divorce his wife if I would just say the word.

Now it was my turn to be the sane one in our relationship.

"No, it would never work," I said.

"Why not?" Brad asked me, in the soft lights of a French restaurant.

"Because if you can't make it with the wife you have now, why do you think you'd ever be able to make it with me?"

"You're different," he said huskily, taking my hands in his. "I feel like I can conquer kingdoms when I'm with you. I'll never forget that lilting laugh of yours. It haunts me sometimes, when I least expect it."

"Brad, you don't know what a mixed-up mess I am, that's all," I said as kindly as I could, looking up at the wrinkles in his forehead. Life was getting hard for him, beginning to show in his face. I wondered if my struggles would show in my face by the time I was thirty-eight too.

"Why don't you think it over for a few weeks, Pat? You may change your mind. I'd give you a good life; we'd travel a lot."

"No, I won't change my mind, Brad. One of these days I suppose I'll end up getting married, but I'll just have to start from scratch with another beginner like myself, I think. You see, I don't want it on *my* conscience that I broke up your marriage. I guess I have some scruples left too."

Years later I picked up a famous national magazine and saw an article on Brad (not his real name, of course). He had achieved singular success with investments, having left his field, and he now had five children instead of the two he'd had when I knew him. I like to think this was an indication that he finally was successful in his marriage too.

During the year that I last saw Brad (1953), I drifted on the most turbulent course of my whole life. I dated two architects, one British and one Italian. For a few weeks I felt I was in love with the British one, while the Italian felt he was in love with me. Eventually, of course, through a humorous set of circumstances, these two met each other and began to compare notes. The English boy dropped me like a hot cake, and I dropped the Italian.

I worked that year as an editorial assistant for an architectural magazine. Gwen, a junior editor at the desk nearest mine, watched wistfully while I went through a bewildering array of boyfriends. After the young architects, there was an old college classmate; after him, a young engineer whom I actually married following a courtship of exactly nine weeks.

Before my engagement, I began to notice that Gwen had real emotional problems. She would stop her work and stare off aimlessly, or sometimes stare at me in a very hostile fashion, her face bathed in jealously. The pressure of dead-lines was too much for her; and she would talk to the senior editors in a funny, squeaky little voice when they came by to see how she was doing as the time approached to put an issue to bed.

My boss asked me a few questions about her behavior one day, and I did have to admit that she was strange at times. But her strangeness did not prepare me for what he told me about her. Someone on the staff lived in an apartment near hers and heard her shrieking out in terror at night; her work had deteriorated to the point that the magazine was going to have to let her go.

I can remember how I felt that night as I went home on the train. What if I did not appeal to men, were a little older, and still unmarried? Would my own dark moods overtake me completely? Would I become an emotional casualty in this overwrought age too?

More than anything else, the fear of some similar fate drove me to accept Dick's proposal of marriage that spring. After all, he said he loved me. And I loved him too, in a way—that is, if I was really capable of love. I had strong doubts about this, but I kept them to myself. We were at-tracted to each other physically, at any rate; and like most young people, it was easy to call that love.

With my characteristic optimism and appetite for fantasy, I decided to give marriage a whirl. One day after Dick and I got back from the beach, he decided to tell my folks about our plans and ask for their permission to marry me. They liked Dick, but they did not share our enthusiasm for a quickie wedding in about three weeks.

"What's the rush?" my Dad pointedly asked Dick.

"Well, sir, we want to get married. And it looks like I'll be going into the service very soon; so I want to be able to take Pat with me."

"Why not wait just six months and see if you both feel the same then, especially Pat?"

I began to get uneasy. My folks knew me so well that they suspected this might just be another one of my phases. Already I was beginning to think they might be right, and it annoyed me to think that they knew better what to do in the situation than I did.

"No!" I said petulantly. "I'm not going to wait around for him at all. Either I marry him now, or we'll just forget the whole thing."

"That we are not going to do," Dick said firmly. "We are going to get married."

The day before our wedding, we took a bike ride up to Crocheron Park near where I lived. As we looked out over the countryside from a high point in the hilly section of the park, I had a shattering experience. Words suddenly came from nowhere, whether from within me or without I don't know, but I heard them. They said, "Don't do it!" There was an urgency and a finality about them which terrified me.

I told Mother about the warning as soon as I got home and asked her what I should do. She looked troubled, but did not know how to advise me. After all, cold feet were common for those about to be brides, were they not? Arrangements were all made for the wedding. Did I really want to change all that?

In a flash of misery I threw myself on the bed, weeping until I was emotionally spent. How could I tell her that I really did not know *what* I wanted, that I had no idea whether this marriage would work or not? Changing things seemed like too big a job to tackle that weary afternoon; so a wedding there was.

On our honeymoon I began to wonder, *What on earth did I ever do this for?* Under such clouds we set out on the stormy sea of our early married life.

4
Encounter with Christ

Like so many others who act just as impulsively, I soon found out that marriage was no instant solution to all of my problems. Rather, it had introduced another complexity into life: how do you make sense out of a maze of seemingly purposeless existence when there is another in it with you who has no answers either?

Dick soon found out that I liked to talk constantly about things in which he had no interest. I soon found out that he could fall asleep in a chair at any time, day or night—especially when I was talking. Although my life was a temperamental yo-yo of ups and downs, at least there *were* the ups. Somehow with Dick's calm-voiced, stealthy-stepped approach, any kind of enthusiasm was suspect.

Dinner time had always been the highlight of the day for me. No matter how simple the fare, my family had always enjoyed a lavish diet of good conversation. My parents, brother and I lived in the realm of ideas, and stimulating rapport between us over the years had established a pattern of thinking things through, especially around the dinner table. Dick, on the other hand, felt the food was the primary purpose for being at the table, and he liked "the cold things cold, and the hot things hot." His family was a large one of hungry boys, each of whom liked to eat and made a fairly serious business of getting his share.

By the time our first son was born, our relationship had become an unpredictable geyser, boiling constantly underneath with seething resentment and subject to frequent violent eruptions in the form of bitter arguments. The only happy times I knew were when we entertained friends and escaped the prison of our togetherness. Gregarious and outgoing, I liked to have company and had grown up in a home where this was a way of life. It came as a rude awakening that Dick did not enjoy guests and somehow felt threatened by the easy way I talked with people. He was especially boorish when the husband of a friend would chat easily with me, and it finally dawned on me that he was jealous. This infuriated me, and the winter scene of my soul became a mass of resentful icicles ready to crash down on both of us at any time and wreck our home.

When Charlie was a year old, we gathered that both our families would be happier to see us apart than together. My mother, in her typical frank way, simply said, "It seems to me you two had better get a divorce before you destroy this child emotionally by your terrible bickering." Dick's mother was more subtle. She just wrote of the marriages of friends or relatives who were breaking up and commented, "They're still young. They can each make a new life for themselves."

The idea began to hold a powerful attraction for me. Why not be done with this mess anyway? Why all the Victorian nonsense about "once married, always married" or the vows we had taken "till death do us part"? I was already busy planning my own life and had embarked on a graduate program of psychology at the University of California. Like so many others who become interested in that field, I hoped I might find some answers to my own problems in the process of learning how to straighten out everyone else.

My dream bubble was short-lived however. Early in the fall of 1956 I realized that I was pregnant again. With the news came a moment of truth. It finally occurred to me that we might well be in too deep to get out, and some solution would have to be found to our problems. It was then that I really began to seek God.

Dick and I had been brought up in a liberal church where no one seemed to think seriously about spiritual things. For years I had known that if I were ever to find God at all, it would probably not be in this church. However, knowing no other place to go, we usually ended up attending services of that denomination whenever we settled in a community.

In our church in Concord, California, I met a sparkling girl a few years older than I who seemed to have some answers. She talked about "not knowing what it was all about until a few years ago" and "seeing the light" one day, apparently rather suddenly. We became close friends and found a few others who were searching for more reality in their lives. During the fall of 1956, we started a weekly Bible study, for Jane had given us the novel idea that this book had some answers. We decided to go through the gospel of Mark at the rate of a chapter a week—simply because it was shortest.

Looking back on those days now, it seems incredible that God could have met any of us. We were pooling our ignorance much more than trying to find out what the Scriptures had to say. However a girl named Ginny came once in a while, and she was different from the rest of us. She talked of *knowing* the Lord and told us we needed to be born again. That sounded like nonsense to me, but it was hard to forget. The annoying words kept popping into my mind at the oddest times, as well as another verse I'd heard somewhere, "Abraham believed God, and it was reckoned to him as righteousness" (Ro. 4:3).

At about this time, my parents were writing heated letters from the East coast complaining about my younger brother, Bill, who had "become a fanatic." He was a student at Cornell and was not doing any of the "normal" things that I had done in college. He did not join a fraternity, never went to dances, and could not even enjoy a good cocktail like the rest of us! His unforgivable move, however, had apparently been getting involved with a "wildly fanatical" group known as Inter-Varsity Christian Fellowship. Quite clearly they were going to ruin him.

Our curiosity was greatly aroused by these letters. (What was a fanatic anyway?) Dick decided to take his vacation at Christmas time that year, and we went East to see both families. We knew that Bill would be home from school, and we could observe him for ourselves.

A few hours after our plane landed, I began to wonder what had gotten into my folks. One thing was certain: Bill was not crazy, and if he were a fanatic, I began to hope it would prove catching. He had always been the sanest, steadiest member of our family—a "good boy" during all the years when I was the "spoiled brat." Even though I had picked on him when he was little, I began to appreciate him mightily during my turbulent college years when he could be an understanding listener. He knew he had a neurotic wildcat for a sister, but he seemed to be able to love me in spite of it.

Mother and dad's behavior toward Bill puzzled me. They picked on him constantly, but often while they were lambasting him, he would be in the midst of doing something kind and thoughtful for them. I remember one day when Mother was sounding off to Bill about something, he was down on his knees scrubbing her kitchen floor for her—without being asked. Never in all my life had I scrubbed a floor unless I had to. If she had spoken to me like that in the midst of such a labor of love, I would have dumped the bucket over right in the middle of the floor and walked out!

That night Bill and I washed the dishes together. It was just like old times, except that he told me I was not a Christian, and this rankled me. We talked late into the night, long after everyone else had gone to bed.

Still a voracious reader, I had taken an interest in Gandhi during the previous year and had read seven biographies about him in my restless search for truth. I monopolized the conversation for quite awhile and finally summarized my views expansively.

"Bill, if Gandhi wasn't 'saved,' as you put it, then no one will ever be. He was one of the best men who ever lived."

My brother answered me, as he often did, with a question.

"Pat, if you were in an airplane at 40,000 feet, could you tell the difference between a well-dressed man and a bum in rags down on the ground?"

"How many feet?"

"Forty thousand."

"No, I guess not. But what's the point?"

"Well, that's a little like it is with God. He's holy and perfect, and from the standpoint of perfect righteousness, he's well above 40,000 feet looking down on the rest of us. The Bible says 'all our righteousness is as filthy rags' to Him. God looks down on a Gandhi or a Genghis Khan and sees very little difference when compared to His *perfect* goodness."

This was a new thought to me. After Bill went to bed I sat and thought about some of the things he had said. What I did not know until much later was that our talk had discouraged him so much that he fell on his knees and wept for me when he got to his room.

Just three weeks after my brother and I had that talk, I sat alone one night in front of the fireplace in my California home. Bill had suggested I read the gospel of John and a history of the Reformation. I had the latter on my lap and found much of it dull going. I was beginning to wonder why he asked me to do such an absurd thing, when I came to the life of John Huss.

Inside me there was a revolution going on while I read the account of his being burned at the stake. He was described as unwavering in his faith, with joy and comfort for others as he was led to his doom. I looked into the fire in front of me and contemplated what it must have felt like to die in that way.

"Lord, I don't believe it," I said suddenly, right out loud.

"No man could die under those circumstances in the way that he did. Any human being would fall apart in a situation like that. I don't care what this book says."

In the silence I became aware of that annoying Bible verse, "You must be born again." *Could* it be that inside Huss there was some kind of divine life which could not be snuffed out by either fear or flames? Was that what it meant to be born again?

Slowly I put the book down and looked in the fire once more. Then an amazing thing happened: I, who had been an agnostic in college, knew in that moment that both heaven and hell were real. Just as shutting my eyes would not stop the fire in my fireplace from burning, so rationalizing about the existence of hell would not stop its being there. Suddenly hell was terribly real and yawning to swallow me up forever unless something happened to change me. Obnoxious habits which bound me with invisible chains rose up before me like the ghost of Christmas past. My stark failure in every area of life suddenly made a mockery of my studied mask of success.

"Lord Jesus," I whispered, "whatever it is you do to people to change them and keep them from going to hell, do it to me."

In that moment a magnificent peace came over me, a glorious sense of having been long away and finally coming home. In that instant, the agony of a thousand nightmares was swept out of my life by the cleansing power of the blood of Christ reaching me on one gigantic wave of God's love. The Lord Jesus captured my heart in one still second, launching me on an endless sea of Life.

From that day to this, a magnificent *person*, Jesus, has been at the very center of my existence, my primary reason for greeting every new day. Although I have failed Him many times, He has never failed me. Even the worst of my backslidings has only served to bring me more utterly to His feet in love and praise; for life without His smile upon it is as hollow as wedding confetti without any bridegroom.

Waves of joy kept settling over me as I slipped into bed,

and I woke Dick up on an impulse. He looked at me a little wildly when I said I had been born again, said, "What?" and then turned over and went back to sleep. I lay there for a long time, hating to have this day end and half afraid that I would wake up in the morning to find it all a dream.

The days that followed showed me much more had happened than a comet's appearance in the dark winter night of my life. In the words of 2 Corinthians 5:17, "Therefore if any man is in Christ, he is a new creature; the old things have passed away; behold, new things have come." *Light* was being diffused through all my days, answering questions and settling enigmas, especially in the Bible—now a brand new book to me. It seemed I never could get enough of it, and that insatiable urge to read which had been with me since childhood was now all channeled toward this one mine of truth. Every answer I had looked for elsewhere, I could dig out here. Many delusions I had clung to in my darkness began to be exposed for what they really were.

Two or three weeks after my conversion, something happened which showed how wonderfully the Lord Jesus Christ had changed my life. Dick had to take a business trip, and the only flight he could get was a midnight departure from San Francisco airport. This meant I had to drive home in the wee hours of the morning after putting him on the plane, and then face the loneliness and fears which were my lot whenever I was left alone at night. Although I never admitted it to anyone, when Dick was away I used to lie awake in terror until the first rays of dawn signaled that it was "safe" to sleep.

Driving back over the Bay Bridge, through the tunnel, and out toward Walnut Creek and home, I assured the Lord that I was a hopeless case. If He could just forgive me for my foolishness, I promised Him I would keep secret forever that I ever went through such agonies. I told him I knew lying there all night listening for noises did not show victory—maybe I'd just sit up and read my Bible until dawn!

Once I got home and into bed, there was a strong inner conviction that I should simply turn off my light and close my eyes. To my amazement when I opened them, the bright morning sunlight was pouring in through our open bathroom door. Jesus had freed me from fear of the dark and of being alone which had bound me since childhood—and I hadn't even asked Him to do it!

Why, if Dick were to come to the Lord, we would really have it made. Surely no couple could have any problems if *both* of them knew the Lord—or so I thought then. That morning watching the sunlight bathe my room, I prayed in a new way for my husband's conversion. "Lord," I whispered, "do *anything* you have to to bring Dick to yourself. We can't go on like this with his walking out of the room every time I talk about You."

That was in February. Early in May, God answered in a surprising way when Dick lost his job. He had been hired to assist a brilliant research scientist in the nuclear field, who died suddenly after contracting chicken pox from his children. Since the specific research project my husband worked on died with Dick Fayram, so did Dick's job.

There was no problem in getting another job, but God used the shock to Dick's ego to bring him to Himself. One night Dick realized, lying in bed, that without God he was even unable to provide for his family. He committed his life to the Lord and invited Him in to take over.

Before long Dick was grabbing for his Bible when he came home from work in the evening. It was my only way of knowing that anything had happened in his life for a while, but in time he was able to talk about it a little.

We began to have an air of expectancy about our lives, as if just around the corner lay a whole new life. One evening, driving home from a supermarket, I watched the sunset with a flash of insight. A day never dies without the promise of a fresh, untried dawn. The golden rays, the red and purple glory, all seemed to say goodbye to one kind of life and hello to a new one, soon to follow.

5

Discovering the Snare

Soon after my sunset premonition, Dick was transferred to the east coast with Western Electric. The warm glow of our life in the golden West all waned in a frenzy of last minute details. That part of our life ended when the train, the City of San Francisco, departed from Oakland station one January afternoon in 1958. As I waved a tearful goodbye to Roland and Eleanore Smith, who would handle unfinished tasks such as getting our car loaded for shipment, I wondered why I had been so eager for a new life. These friends and others like them had warmly welcomed us into the family of God; it was heart-wrenching to leave them.

The first day out I did nothing but care for our two little boys (one with an ear infection which did not improve his disposition) and huddle in the corner of our compartment to cry. I hardly spoke to Dick, whom I blamed for this hard move. With typical feminine lack of logic, I conveniently forgot that I had urged him to take this job despite the transfer to the East.

Gone were the fresh peaches from the the garden, the easy

patio life, and the warm Christian fellowship of the evangelical church we had joined. Ahead lay a confrontation with our families who were hostile to the gospel, and an introduction into a new kind of neighborhood, the indifferent aloof environment of the New York City suburbs.

Two and a half days after we left California, we arrived at our destination. The beauty of the Rockies and the Great Plains were soon forgotten in the maze and cluttered rush of eastern urgency. In a state of rude shock we floundered like blind moles on a subterranean level of Grand Central Station. Bewildered, I tried to clutch my children close as Dick grabbed the luggage and tried to stay with us in the mob scene.

Someone had said that God, like a great eagle with her young, will jolt His children out of a comfortable nest to teach them to fly. That bleak January day I desperately wanted wings to fly, little dreaming how long the cold winter would be that lay just ahead. God's greatest mercy is the unwritten page of the future and His grace the pen that writes the present.

Life soon became a series of dilemmas which were hard to resolve. If we were "saved," our families reasoned, why did they find so many things about our lives hard to take? What was the cause of the wall between us—God? If I had been mightily changed, why did I still have the same nasty temper? (I did still have it, much as I hated to admit it.) Why was our marriage no better than before? (It wasn't; in fact, there were days in 1958 and 1959 when I began to suspect it was really worse.) We had found another good evangelical church and were getting to know some fine friends; why was I lonely and restless so much of the time?

Any young mother who has nursed preschoolers through a domino string of winter illnesses in a new neighborhood will have some idea of how I felt that spring of 1958. It seemed I had left the sunshine of my life behind in California. Without great success, I spent much of my time fighting off severe depression as unreasonable and persistent as it was deadening. My main attack was a frenetic approach to life which left me few idle moments to think, for I recognized even then that my idle thought life got me into considerable trouble.

Reading, telephoning, house work, and the care of the children did not do the job. My moods got darker and lasted longer without relief. I begged Dick to let me get a job somewhere, for I feared I might be heading for real emotional trouble. In his easygoing way, he let me take a job as a social worker for a state hospital though my earnings barely paid for the cost of a baby sitter and transportation. (I had the experience required to serve in a temporary capacity until a psychiatric social worker could be found.)

Those few months at Marlboro State Hospital in central New Jersey taught me what no experienced Christian had ever mentioned to me: the real and terrible condition of a human personality under the control of *another* personality. The frequency of a phrase repeated on many of the case histories shocked me. If it's just a *delusion* of demon possession, I reasoned, why do so many patients have the same delusion?

In my innermost thoughts I suspected that the occasional unearthly shriek from the disturbed ward had no earthly source. One day, since the nurse on the epileptic ward was not at her desk, I had to walk the whole long corridor to the other end in order to deliver a message. Halfway down the hall, I heard a gutteral, middle-aged, man's voice utter a horrible obscenity. Looking into the doorway, I saw no man at all—only a four-year-old girl who was in the room alone, and who leered at me in the most terrible way I had ever seen.

That experience turned on a light of understanding which would never again go out. What the Bible calls demon possession is still with us today, and any attempt to distort or whitewash this fact will only render those trying to cope with it impotent to do so. While I worked in that hospital I heard a psychiatrist say, "You know there is no cure for mental illness." But I slipped my Bible out of my desk and noticed that there was a sure cure for demon possession.

The evil spirits were always cast out by the Lord or by believers in the name of the Lord.

Here I faced one of the dilemmas of those years of painful revelation: would it still work? The Bible said it would. In fact it was to be a kind of credential to show the believer was for real. "And these signs will accompany those who have believed: in My name they will cast out demons" (Mark 16:17). Yet the Christians we knew never so much as mentioned the possibility; indeed, there was apparently general agreement that this was a forbidden subject.

Despite the need all around me, I never tried to find out if demon powers could be vanquished in Jesus' name. A psychiatric social worker was found, my temporary job came to an end, and I resumed my role as wife, mother and homemaker. The change had helped me a great deal, and I slipped into an active role in our church with new vigor.

We were now in an environment with excellent Bible teaching and a strong emphasis on missions. Gradually I came to believe that the most complete commitment to the Lord Jesus Christ was a life offered to foreign missions. I prayed for a year that Dick would see this too, and one day in the fall of 1959, he came home from a business trip announcing that God had dealt with him about turning his back on worldly opportunity and volunteering for missionary service.

Those were exciting days. The following summer we sold our home, Dick quit his fine job, and with our two boys we left for Columbia Bible College in South Carolina. Two years later we landed in Kano, Nigeria, as new missionaries, attending language school, sent by an interdenominational group.

After being in Nigeria just about six weeks, our tiny baby daughter, Beth Ann (born just five weeks before we left the United States), and I came down with severe cases of malaria. We were flown to a mission hospital in Jos, several hundred miles south of Kano, where each of us made a slow recovery.

One night there in Jos as I looked over at my baby's crib,

I began to shake with something more than malarial chills. A nameless fear took hold of me, and I wondered if we had done the right thing to come to Africa after all. Before this experience of serious illness, I had given little thought to the idea of a personal devil. I knew the Scriptures pictured Satan as a rebel fallen from heaven because of mutiny against God and that he was now in charge of a whole vast evil army which included fallen angels and demons.

For the five years since our conversion to Christ, these facts had had no more effect on Dick and me than facts we had learned in history books. It never occurred to us that we could be subject to malicious purposes from this source. My fear now owed itself to the same kind of insight I had received the night of my conversion. Hell was real; so was satanic opposition.

The fear that came with this understanding was indescribable. I shuddered from head to foot. Not even the seven blankets I already had on the bed helped ease those chills. My teeth chattered in quick staccato rhythm, while my fingernails dug deep into my elbows in my futile attempt to pull myself together.

Then, strangely, all was peace. I was aware of God speaking directly to my heart—not in an audible voice, but with the distinct impression of words stamped upon some inner consciousness. The message was *Don't ever fear the devil again.* A warmth spread through my body which now lay still. Somewhere in my memory a Scripture verse came forcibly to mind, "The Son of God appeared for this purpose, that He might destroy the works of the devil."

Suddenly it dawned on me that the Lord had suffered the agony of Calvary and had broken the power of death in his own resurrection not *only* to save us from our sins, but to give us victory in Him over any attack the forces of evil could launch against us. That night I saw that it was God's will for His children to be victors in every trial of life; we were never to find ourselves in a situation for which we were not equal.

I saw these things rationally; however, it was to be a long time before I experienced the reality of these facts in my own life. My most difficult courses in God's school lay ahead, and they were all required. Thank God that He is patient and can wait for us to stumble and be covered with mud, never to forget His own matchless way of washing it away.

The months following language school held many puzzling experiences, especially for an analytical thinker like me. As we settled into teaching for a mission secondary school, several facts became painfully obvious. One of these was that the missionaries we worked with were not spiritual giants; they were simply stumblers, frequently bunglers, like us. An even more unpleasant reality was that our private lives were worse in Africa than at home. My temper was more volatile than ever, and before very long nothing Dick could do was right.

The dichotomy in my life became a great, searing pain to me; I was aware of it all the time. I could get up in chapel and give a powerful devotional message on Scripture made real to my heart by God, but I found it impossible to love those around me. All I could see in the students was their desperate lack of real spiritual life, and all they could see in me were inconsistencies and the contrast between my talk and my walk. I lived in terror that some student might pass our home and hear me verbally tearing my husband apart; yet I had no respect for the many missionaries whose calm extended to lack of real zest and enthusiasm for the Lord. Many seemed to be weary spokes in a gigantic wheel which had long since lost its reason for turning, hard put to find a reason for its existence.

I noticed a pattern which repeated itself on each of the three stations where we worked. In each area there existed relationships between missionaries which were not right, no matter how charitable the assessment. Resentments were deep and often of long standing, usually dating back to some trivial incident. The rest of the workers on the station were inevitably affected by the adverse climate brought about by these strong feelings, and a game was played called "cover up."

The rules of this game were easy to learn. Before long I

could have written the *Hypocrite's Handbook* myself. The contents might go something like this. Rule 1: Pretend it isn't so that A hates B. We are to love one another; therefore, assume love to be a fact. Rule 2: Never let the pot come to a full boil, it might boil over. Who knows what might happen if we said what we think? Rule 3: Remember we are here to give the good news of the gospel to these people. At all costs put up a brave front before them. This is part of our cross. They'll never know how hard it is. (Or will they? That was the nagging fear.) Rule 4: Never admit you are wrong. Rule 5: Do not speak up in opposition to the station or mission leadership. Remember, if you do not see the reason for a procedure now, the time will come in future years when you will see things as they do. (This was, at times, a goal to make one shudder!)

Of course, it would be unfair to present just one side of the picture. There are radiant souls in missionary service who serve from an inexhaustible supply of love and joy from deep within. Their lives are characterized by spontaneity and buoyant energy which is baffling to others. Everywhere they go, they love (easily, effortlessly), passing on the warmth to others from the hidden resources of the Holy Spirit within.

One question that bothered me more and more was this: was it possible to start out with spontaneous joy and love and then have it disappear? Weren't the motives of most commendable in the beginning? What happens to someone who wants to serve the Lord with all his heart, but ends up compromising, insipid, and consumed by the fear of man? I was not yet sure of the answer, but one thing I did know, "An enemy has done this" (Matthew 13:28).

6
Caught in the Snare

It was about ten o'clock one still, sultry evening in the small west African bush town where we lived, time to decide whether to go to bed before the electricity went off or to stay up and light the kerosene pressure lamp.

There was a soft knock at our door, and a young national stood there holding his hand against his chest, pleading with his fear-ridden eyes. My husband asked him if he'd been hurt, and a dazed face looked up at him.

"Not exactly, but there's something in here that worries me all the time," the boy said softly. "The dispensary isn't open. I wonder if you can help me?"

Dick's answer was firm.

"I'm sorry, but we are not medical missionaries. We cannot help, and you'd better go before it is too late to find a place to stay in the village."

The boy's bewildered face fell. Slowly, reluctantly he turned and left our porch, his hand still pressed against his short-sleeved white shirt. His navy blue shorts clearly identified him as a secondary student in uniform. I wondered where he went to school and walked out on the porch to ask him, but it was too late. The station power plant went off, and he was swallowed up in the inky night.

Oh, if only I knew which way he had gone, so I could run after him and bring him back! There was an eerie quality about him, as if he were enveloped by strange powers of darkness. Why couldn't we snatch him from them?

"Why did you send him away?" I flung at my husband as he opened the door for me and handed me a flashlight. Dick was usually a good listener with students. Why had he so quickly dismissed someone who obviously needed help?

There was a loud hiss as the pressure lamp went on, and Dick looked up at me in surprise.

"Didn't you hear the radio this morning? There was a warning about a runaway secondary student, deranged and potentially dangerous, who is visiting homes of 'Europeans' in the area, ostensibly to get help for his chest. He is a thief."

"I don't care. That look in his eyes, that pain in his chest, that 'something in there' that worries him all the time. He has demons, I just know it. Why can't we help him?"

There was no answer to my question, but I hardly expected any. After all, it was a rhetorical one anyhow. When had we ever helped anyone with demons before?

I picked up the flashlight again and went into our bedroom. As I tucked the edges of our mosquito net under the mattress, my mind was seething with unanswered questions. Why were we out here anyway? Weren't we supposed to snatch people "from the domain of darkness" and see them transferred "to the kingdom of His beloved Son" if we were really working for God?

What if this boy *were* demon oppressed? Were we to fear such people, such demons—we who are in Christ? I knew the Bible stated flatly, "The Son of God appeared for this purpose, that He might destroy the works of the devil" (1 John 3:8). Were the children of the King to be sniveling cowards when confronted with the unseen minions of Satan? If retreat from the battle is permissible, why is there no armor for the back in God's mighty arsenal of Ephesians 6?

In deep revulsion against what we had done, I slipped to my knees, covering my face with my hands as the flood gates broke. The Word of God stabbed my heart with the verse that had disturbed me in my days at Marlboro State Hospital. Long shunned and deliberately overlooked, the unwelcome words forced themselves upon my thoughts, "And these signs will accompany those who have believed: in My name they will cast out demons. . . ."

God is the master teacher of all His required courses. If He has decided it is time for us to learn a truth, He has ways of making sure we pass. (We may even get an A before we finish all our exams!) I was to find the answers to all my perturbing questions in God's jungle camp, my own personal experience.

Even before that brief, haunting encounter with the troubled secondary student, I had been having some rather novel experiences in prayer. "Leadings" about the future came to me almost like whispers in the soul. A few of these proved accurate as time went on, which made me think God had given me some kind of prophetic gift. Bible verses were often skillfully woven into the warp and woof of these ideas, causing me to accept them without question.

Most thrilling of all was waking with a start every morning precisely at five A.M. Some invisible friend or inaudible reveille brought about this compulsive awakening, and of course I felt it must be the Lord. I had always been a night person and a sluggish riser. How wonderful it was to think that God would wake me up and call me out to the small mud hut near the house for these unusual times of prayer.

Guidance was becoming a very specific, detailed matter which took the major portion of the two hour period I was now allotting for my quiet time. At first nothing I was led to do conflicted with what I knew to be right. However as the weeks passed, irrational and questionable behavior was suggested to me, and I found myself under some compulsion to obey. My future leadings became quite grim, and there was a decided preoccupation with prophecies concerning death in our immediate family.

Dick wondered why these long prayer times were not doing me any good, for invariably I would come in for breakfast at seven o'clock in a poor mood. My irritability and ill temper were hard on him and the children, and he tried to talk to me about the problem once or twice. Yet I rationalized everything so cleverly, to myself and to him, that neither of us felt I was in any kind of danger. The climate, my frail constitution, and something I liked to call my "temperate zone artistic temperament" were responsible for my poor disposition. I still wince as I remember the lengths to which I went to try to convince the Africans that I had some built-in excuse for blowing my top.

Soon my health began to fail, and within a few short months I had lost thirty-five pounds and landed in the hospital. There were some painful, hard lumps under my right arm, which were removed and sent to the United States for biopsy analysis. My illness was tentatively diagnosed by a mission doctor as mononucleosis. Later the American pathologist wrote her that he had found parasites suggestive of toxoplasmosis, a disease of the lymph glands.

During the three months after I got back from the hospital, I became severely anemic and suffered from several respiratory infections. It was as though an invisible destroyer were weaving a gigantic web about me from which there was no escape. I had to forego my early morning watch in the outside hut, for I was now spending much of each day in bed, but the strange leadings still persisted.

One day, as I was struggling to hang up a small wash on the line, I was aware of a voice saying to me, "Today you shall be with me in paradise." I knew these were the words of Jesus on the cross to the repentant thief. Therefore never questioned—God must have been the one speaking to me. In my confusion I interpreted this to mean that would die before midnight. With great effort because of my extreme weakness, I stumbled around doing things suitable for one's last few hours here on earth. I wrote letters to few people I had wronged years ago, begging forgiveness. I utterly dumbfounded our African cook by confessing my angry outbursts of temper as sin.

At bedtime I spent an hour or so rehearsing my many marital failures and begging Dick anxiously to forgive me for them. After he fell into a bewildered sleep, I lay there in corpselike rigidity, awaiting my death and assuring myself of eternal glory soon to be experienced.

After a while it seemed that I had waited long enough, so I took out the flashlight we kept between our pillows and shined it on the alarm clock on the big desk across the room. To my amazement it was nearly one o'clock, and I was still very much alive! This shock would have been enough to kill me if I had had a weak heart. As I lay there in the dark, I began to face the first of many unpleasant realities. *That voice lied to me,* I thought. *That means it could not have been God, for the Bible says that God cannot lie. Who is doing this to me?*

My answer was horrible laughter which I heard as if far off in the distance. Then I heard a few snatches of music in a minor key played by an orchestra, and I called out, "Lord, help me!" Immediately all sounds stopped, and in a very few minutes I fell into a fitful sleep.

Nine thousand miles away in Oxford, Maryland, a friend was suddenly burdened to pray for me. Several times in the last few weeks Betty Wilford had awakened suddenly from a sound sleep with a deep burden for me. This particular evening she had not gone to bed yet, but she had an overwhelming conviction that I was in dire need. Wave upon wave of anxiety swept over her as she thought of me, and then she heard herself praying, "Lord, send Pat home. Oh Lord, I don't know what it is, but I have a terrible feeling that she can't survive out there. Move anything or anyone you have to, Lord, but *send Pat home!*"

Ten days later, just after dark, I found myself boarding a huge Pan Am jet liner at Lagos airport with little four-year-old Beth Ann clutching my right hand. On my left, a handsome young Nigerian airline official carried our ten-month-old baby, Billy, and the diaper bag and other essentials I was taking aboard. God sent his angel to me that day, crisply efficient and warmly compassionate in his Nigerian Airlines uniform. He had apparently just gotten off duty and found me sitting dazed and helpless in the airline waiting room, having just arrived from Jos. I was wondering how, without a porter in sight, we could get to the international terminal at least a mile away. Dick had worried about this when I left him in Bauchi. We knew that missionaries would be there to help me in the big terminal, but what if I had a problem getting there or finding them? I had said noncha-lantly, "Oh, the Lord will send some man along to help me out like He has all my life."

Here he was, grinning down at me as I huddled with my various bags and babies. I could have thrown my arms around him and kissed him.

The next few hours were a miracle of details cared for while I sat like a delighted fairy princess and watched. My knight paid the airport tax for me, handled all my customs arrangements, got special permission for me to board early, and personally escorted me and the children to our seats. The missionaries were there all right, but would have been helpless to do any of the things I was too weak to do since it required an official uniform to get in all those places, unless one were a ticketed passenger.

As soon as we were aboard, my special angel in uniform disappeared as quickly as he had appeared, and I never even asked his name. I began to cry a little, realizing that now I could not even write his company and thank them for his infinite kindness to me, when an odd thought occurred to me: perhaps he was a real angel and had already vanished from that airport scene. (When I get to heaven, this is one of the first questions I am going to ask God.)

As the fairyland lights of the largest all black city in Africa twinkled a merry farewell behind us, tears streamed down my face from tight shut eyes. With childish charm Beth Ann waved with both hands, her nose pressed against the window of the jet. Billy was already peacefully asleep, his tiny face snuggled against my shoulder. My arms were locked about him, the warmth from that dear form the only reassuring feeling of those awful moments. I had come to this land with such bright hopes, such a sheer longing to serve my Lord and be of some use to Him; now I was slinking home, three months before the end of our term, a medical emergency. Two mission doctors had felt that I might not survive the dry season, and here I was fleeing at their orders.

As I looked back over the four years in Africa, one word branded itself across my mind, searing its way into my thoughts: *failure.* I had failed as a missionary, as a teacher, as a wife and mother, and even as a person. I was a shell of the bounding, exuberant optimist who had flown west across the same ocean fours years before.

Deep down within me I knew I was finished as a missionary, that I would never go back. As I opened my eyes and looked down at the frail, skeletal wrists resting on my baby's back, I wondered if I would ever live to start over again. Could God write a new chapter in a life like mine, or had His *finis, the end* been written just a few leaves before the conclusion of my life?

7
Surely He Shall Deliver

As the big jet circled for its New York landing in sunless, drab smog, I felt a sinking sensation within me—grim reality settling around delusions long nurtured by my strange leadings. It was a gray, rainy day at the international airport, but not half as gray or shrouded as my own soul.

Unsettling flashbacks of what I had been when I left home startled me into sudden honesty as I fastened seat belts for our landing. Where was the zeal that would not let a day go by without at least one person spoken to about Jesus? Where were the sense of humor, the boundless energy, the characteristic hope and enthusiasm, the concern for how other people felt?

Billy clung to me as I held the compact with the arm that encircled him and combed my hair with the other hand. Almost in disbelief I saw as for the first time scraggly hair fitly crowning my emaciated frame. The deep circles under the dour, hopeless eyes were frightening to me. Could this shell of a human being, indeed, be *me?*

That moment of rare honesty was only one of the dozens

of flashes of insight the Spirit of God used in the weeks that followed to bring me back from the never-never-land of satanic bondage into which I had wandered. There was my mother's agonized shriek of shock when she first saw me. There was the terse, tight-lipped silence of my father, who had predicted our African service would be suicidal. Jesus once said, "You shall know the truth, and the truth shall make you free," and He was beginning the long process of delivering me "from the snare of the fowler."

The next few weeks gave me a sordid, full view of the horrible pit into which I had fallen. There were the stunned reactions of old friends when they first saw my emaciated frame. Then there was constant nausea, peculiar tremors, and an awful buzzing in the ears. Once there was an ominous *gong* which seemed to sound from my innermost being and point out that indeed the bell had tolled for me. In that moment when waves of inexplicable fear gripped me, I cried to the Lord either to deliver me from this living hell or to take me home to Him.

One day I went to a tea in a lovely home in Annapolis, Maryland, where I was to be the speaker to a group of women who were hungry for God. Just before I started to share the Lord with them, the smiling, encouraging faces faded, and a kind of swirling blackness enveloped me. Suddenly my mind turned blank; my body became faint. An invisible vise kept my lips shut tight, and I could say nothing. In desperation I repeated the name of Jesus over and over in my mind. Just as suddenly, the terrible blackness lifted, and my mouth was released for speech.

With great liberty I spoke on Acts 1:8 for about an hour. Many women were in tears when I finished, and some stayed to ask questions and share experiences for two more hours. Yet as I drove back over the Bay Bridge to my folks' home on the eastern shore, God, who is truth, forced me to ask myself some questions. What had happened to me as the meeting began? What if God had not lifted that awful darkness from me? Why was I in this state? *How could I get out of it?*

God is faithful. I soon learned that the One who strips us of our deceptions so that we can ask the right questions is ready with the right answers. One night my eyes fell on an article in *Christian Life* describing the plight of those caught in a web of demonic torment. It spoke of the awful reality of demonic oppression, vexation, and bondage even in Christian believers. I recoiled in fascination and horror, for everything it described had my name on it.

That night I longed for sleep to ease the shock of this revelation. Just as I became drowsy, a strange, unearthly cry came from my chest. In terror my hands grasped the sides of the bed, and my eyes opened wide. There was no possibility of hallucination, for a vibrating feeling in the same area of the chest accompanied the sound.

My body froze in that terrible moment of insight. My fingers would not close. Yet in that paralysis of the body, my mind had perfect clarity. I confessed every sin I could remember and quoted scripture on the blood of Christ, for I remembered that I had read somewhere that this would help any conflict with the forces of darkness. I pled with the Lord to deliver me from this awful thing, finally falling into an exhausted sleep shortly before dawn.

The next morning, to my utter dismay and revulsion, I realized that I was not yet free. The tremors and buzzing in the ears were still with me. God was teaching me something a multitude of His children are having to learn in these days: one cannot pray or plead away a demon power. It has to be cast out in Jesus' name. Prayer may help, but it will not substitute for the word of command.

What a blow to my pride! This meant I had to find some believers who knew how to cast the demon out of me. It also meant the death of my fond theology that Christians cannot have demons, for I had to admit being prey to them myself.

A few weeks later I found my way to some people who knew how to go to battle against the powers of darkness. With them I began to learn some truths which would change the whole course of my life. They pointed out that in Ephesians 4:27 the Scripture says, "Do not give the devil an opportunity." The prince of darkness can only work where he gets a foothold in the life or where he has never lost it. Two of his favorite loopholes in our personalities are interest in the occult or an attitude of unforgiveness.

This group questioned me closely about any interest I may ever have had in fortune tellers, occult "games," or horoscopes. Ruefully I had to admit that I had played the ouija board as a teenager and from time to time had read horoscopes.

"But when I came to know Christ," I remember protesting, "I put all that behind me! How could I be demonically oppressed because of something that took place long before my conversion?"

"Because you apparently never fully let it go," one of the men said promptly. "You have told us much about getting future leadings in prayer. Do you realize where that stuff comes from? It comes from the pit!"

"But how could it?" I insisted. "When I asked the Lord about things to come, I certainly never for a moment thought the devil would answer my prayers!"

"When your prayers are wrong, you can most certainly get supernatural responses from another source," his wife answered. "It is not healthy or biblical to have a curiosity about the future. God condemns all attempts to seek such information in such passages as Deuteronomy 18:10–14; Isaiah 8:19, 20, and Isaiah 47:10–15."

"Do you mean that God would stay absolutely silent and just let the devil, or that thing in me, talk to me at a time like that?" I asked shakily. The buzzing in my ears was getting louder as I spoke, and the tremor I had noticed recently was much more pronounced, especially in my arms.

"That is just what we mean," she said kindly and with a look of real compassion as I faced my moment of ugly truth. "You have a lying spirit of prophecy in you, and we can cast it out if you will confess this curiosity as sin and tell God you want nothing more to do with it."

I knelt down between the man and his wife. She began to pray and repeat the phrase "the blood of Jesus" over and over again, while he amazed me with a direct verbal attack on Satan and this demon that had plagued me for so long.

Finally he said, "You lying spirit of prophecy come out of her in Jesus' name!"

Immediately a horrible shudder went through my whole body, and convulsive sobs came up from deep within. I could hardly believe that the uncontrollable weeping I heard was mine at all. In actuality, it was not. Later I was to read in Maxwell Whyte's works that these are the demon's crocodile tears on leaving and losing a body through which to express its personality.

Afterward I still felt extremely tense, but I knew there had been a change. Like the Gerasene demoniac, whom the Lord delivered during his earthly ministry, I felt I was sitting, clothed, and in my right mind. That night I slept without any interruption for the first time in many months, and I did not awaken at exactly five A.M. to pray.

Within two weeks I had gained five pounds, and by the end of three months my weight and blood were completely normal. A surprising by-product of my deliverance was that my eyes were healed. I no longer needed the glasses I had worn for years and, like most women, was delighted to have it that way.

However, the most dramatic change in my life was the opening of my spiritual eyes to the nature of the great conflict in which we are all engaged. Suddenly the blinders were gone. The Lord showed me situations as they *were*, and not as I *wished* them to be. The many heartaches of my past began to fall into place. Every incident in life began to have significance in terms of the battle between the Spirit of God and the evil powers of Satan.

When my husband came home from the field, weary from the pressures of life in a land seething with civil war, I had to face another whole series of unpleasant realities. My physical health had improved after my initial deliverance, but I had not improved in my attitude toward him. The storm warnings which were clearly visible when we met at Kennedy International Airport that August day in 1966 became gale warnings in the weeks that followed. I often felt like a small craft being tossed on angry waves of resentment which might at any time dash me against the rocks of divorce.

Like so many others with serious marital problems, I desperately wanted to be a good mother to my four children—but I didn't know whether I could stand living with their father! There were many days in 1966 and 1967 when I was sorry I had lived to see Dick's return from Nigeria.

These were trying days for the whole family: the hollow sham of pretense before our Christian friends, the despicable hypocrisy of acting as though we were considering a second term in Africa, facing the hard, cold facts of our lives as they really were in the privacy of our own thoughts. Like many a missionary wife, I had found that I had married "for better or for worse, but not for lunch." Too much exposure to each other at too frequent intervals had brought out every weakness in our marriage. The idea of any repetition of this togetherness was unthinkable to me.

Another unsettling matter in those days was the keeping of my best prayer-meeting image. What would my evangelical brethren think of me when they knew I had had a demon cast out? Indeed, what would they think when they knew the whole truth, that I probably had a few more which needed to come out! God accurately diagnoses the problem I was having in Proverbs 29:25, "The fear of man brings a snare." The rest of that verse gives His prescription and cure for this disease, "but whoever puts his trust in the Lord shall be safe." I found out it worked only when I finally got the nerve to try it.

Trusting the Lord, in my case, involved being honest about my need for deliverance from demonic oppression. During those two years God branded Revelation 12:11 permanently on my mind: "And they overcame him [Satan] because of the blood of the Lamb and because of the word of their testimony, and they did not love their life even to death."

All around us were Christian friends who appeared to be

caught in a demonic web, desperately trying to find a way to victory. If my testimony would help, did I have any right to hide it from them? God was showing me that there is no *real* alternative to His will—a truth I have had to face many times since. Finally I began to care more for what *He* thought of me than what other believers thought, and I decided to share my experience.

I first dropped my little bomb into the comfortable orthodoxy of a Bible study group I had taught in 1959. We met once a month in 1967 with a different leader for each session, since many of the girls had been teaching groups themselves in the interim. When my turn came to lead, I taught on spiritual warfare and ended the lesson by sharing how God had answered their many earnest prayers for my deliverance during my health crisis.

It came as a great shock to some that God had sent me to people who cast a demon out of me in order to deliver me from ill health. This testimony turned off these friends, and it became evident from then on that some of them were ex-friends.

However a fascinating thing happened. The rest of the girls present that day were turned on by my frank witness. The very next day one of them phoned to ask if she could come and talk with me. I taught her some of the basic things the deliverance prayer group had taught me. Soon she was on her knees pouring out a heartbroken confession to God— her teenage experiences with a ouija board, the idle horoscope reading over a morning cup of coffee, and a hungry devouring of Jeanne Dixon's annual prophecies. When that was over, she wept for several minutes. Then at my urging, she told Satan to get going in Jesus' name.

I wondered at the time whether my friend needed to have any demons cast out, but since we had no experts present, I decided we had better forget that part. Despite my ignorance and unwillingness to do the whole job however, the Lord was gracious to this girl. She smiled freely for the first time in many months before she left. In the weeks that followed she found the heavy depression which had plagued her for years had lifted, and she was better able to cope with some serious marital problems herself.

My second attempt to tell about my deliverance was not so successful. I made an appointment with a pastor who was interested in me as a missionary speaker for his church. He saw nothing wrong with reading the daily horoscope "just like the funny papers" and told me my concern about dabbling in the occult bordered on superstition.

I tried to tell him why these things are so dangerous by sharing with him some of the agony I had gone through as a result of my own ignorance. His eyes narrowed down to grim slits when I told him that a demon had been cast out of me.

With lips etched downward in withering scorn, he shot out in heated defense-of-the-faith rhetoric, "Are you trying to tell me that you, a born again Christian, could have a demon *inside* you? Why, that's heresy, the doctrine of demon possession of the believer. I'd *never* believe that."

"I didn't say I was possessed," I answered him slowly. "Perhaps I was oppressed or obsessed. I was mightily *bothered,* let me tell you, and I'm awfully glad the thing left. As long as it was in me, I couldn't help myself."

"How on earth do you think the Holy Spirit could be in the same body with an evil spirit?" he spat out at me hoarsely. His face was reddening now, and the veins stood out in his neck.

"I don't know, but I strongly suspect that whatever part of my life the demon held had never been yielded to the Holy Spirit. Why does the Bible warn us to 'give no place to the devil' if there is no place we can give?"

"Don't try to distract me with an exercise in logic. Where in the Scripture does it say that a Christian can have a demon?" The pastor jumped to his feet as he said this, looking at his watch.

"Where in the Scripture does it say he can't?" I countered.

The interview was clearly at an end. Smiling at me in a patronizing way, he said, "I'm sorry, but I do have to go now. I promised my wife I'd get home by five, and it's that now."

"I'm sorry this testimony has upset you," I said carefully. "I hope God will not have to teach you this truth at as great a cost as I learned it."

On the way home in the car I had it out with the Lord. "Please forgive me," I whispered. "Lord Jesus, it looks like I blew it. What went wrong?"

There was no audible voice, but suddenly the wonderful peace that I have known just a few times since my conversion settled over me. A strong conviction came that my responsibility was merely to tell it like it is. I could leave the results with Him.

Within one week after this incident, the Lord opened a surprising door in our home church, Long Hill Chapel in Chatham, New Jersey. The teacher of the ladies' class was no longer able to continue her ministry there because of poor health. The superintendent approached me. Would I agree to teach?

Little did he know the turmoil his question aroused in me. Could I ever teach again without including the insights God had given me on the great conflict? If these matters did come up, would I then be rejected by the very believers who meant the most to me? How could I ever deny the *experience* without at the same time denying the Deliverer? I told him I would pray about it, but my initial answer was no. The class went through a series of guest teachers while I fervently prayed that God would send someone permanent to them and resolve my dilemma. The answer to this one came back no. Three months later I was again asked to take the class, and I did, almost begrudgingly. Sooner or later I felt, I would become a controversial figure because of beliefs which many Christians think of as divisive.

By now Dick and I had been forced to resign from the mission we had served, because I had told the leaders that I was delivered from a demon power. This testimony was considered untrue, since anyone properly taught knew that a Christian could not have a demon. This, of course, is where the division always occurs. My first two experiences had already taught me that. When a believer claims to have been delivered from an evil spirit, there will be sharp cleavage among those who hear about it: some will believe it, some will not. If this is divisiveness, then those of us who have experienced deliverance must plead guilty. Like Peter and John before the Sanhedrin, "we cannot stop speaking what we have seen and heard."

On Easter morning of 1968 I faced a real test as I stood before my charming, well-dressed Sunday school class. Several of the women were close friends, and most of them had known and respected me for a decade. God was dealing with me. Would I try to hide the truth about my own deliverance or not?

We had just noted that Mary Magdalene was the first person to see the Lord after his resurrection. I asked the women what particular thing Scripture always mentioned about this girl. To my chagrin, not one of those well-taught, Bible believing sisters in Christ would answer me. The Lord nudged me out of my complacency, and I knew the time had come.

"Well," I could hear my hollow voice saying, "Mary Magdalene had this claim to fame: she had had seven demons cast out of her. I appreciate the fact that Jesus let her be the first one to see Him after He arose from the dead, because I've had a demon cast out of me. Maybe those who have been delivered from such awful darkness have the most appreciative eyes for resurrection life."

Wide eyes stared at me in shocked disbelief from under some brightly flowered bonnets. A few glanced down as if to spare me the embarrassment they knew must be mine. Some looked at me with obvious pity, probably wondering if the African sun had affected my mind. But there were others, as there always are, for whom this testimony came as a first ray of hope in a maze of personal darkness.

In the weeks that followed, there was the predictable flutter of excitement over my strange announcement. One woman left the class with a flourish, stating that she would not "sit under heresy" another minute. Several others dropped out less obtrusively, but the Lord brought new ones to take their places. Soon a crescendo of interest developed about the great conflict between God and Satan, and class members asked me to teach a course on it.

As I began to search, I was amazed at the dearth of good teaching material on the warfare. About the only book I found to be of help for a Bible survey course was *The Invisible War* by Donald Grey Barnhouse. This book was very helpful, but it did not deal with the issue contemporary Christians want faced most squarely: what effect can demons have on believers, and what are we to do about them?

Again the Lord taught me in the one way that always works with those who are willing to learn. Ahead lay more time in the jungle camp of experience. My behavior at home revealed that I was still, at times, at the mercy of demon powers. Perhaps not every reader will have to learn the hard way as I did. My prayer is that those who are at the mercy of a temper or appetite that governs *them* will have the grace to admit it. The shorter the road to deliverance, the less the ordeal for the tormented one and for those who must bear with him.

8
Attack and Counterattack

By the fall of 1968 I was a thoroughly controversial figure. Since there was now nothing to hide, I decided to stop playing the coward, roll up my shirt sleeves, and take the offensive against the devil. After all, he had made a mess of much of my life without any right to do so. I was firmly convinced that Satan *had* been completely defeated by the Lord Jesus on Calvary, and that his primary tactics since then had been devoted to keeping us from finding it out. Why should so many fine people be lying in the dust, moaning under the kicks of earth's bully? I was determined to show them that if they would stand up to him, he would flee as James 4:7 promises.

With gusto I prepared the Bible survey course entitled "The Great Conflict." Then for the sake of some friends who were ready for more, I also taught a class in one of their homes on how to handle satanic deception in our own lives. For this purpose we used Jessie Penn-Lewis's mighty work, *War on the Saints,* which grew out of the Welsh revival. This book will never be popular in hell.

My own popularity in the nether regions fell to its greatest low when I was asked to write a tract on the dangers of occult involvement. From the day that I started to work on this project, chaos was unleashed in my life. Evidently a whole division from the infernal army had been assigned to keep me from finishing. Every time I decided to spend some time on it, I would develop a headache, a fever, or a stomach ache. Usually I ended up going to bed and forgetting the whole thing.

Never before my trouble in 1966 had I had trouble with insomnia. Now I began to have terrifying experiences soon after I went to sleep at night, which left me wide awake for hours. I came to dread the nights and would put off going to bed until very late, lying for quite a while in anxiety after I got there. Typically, I would finally drop off into an exhausted sleep around 1:30 A.M.—only to be rudely awakened a few minutes later by a sense of some harsh voice yammering at me, "You're going to hell. You're going to hell." Wearily I would sit up in bed, my head pounding, trying to pull myself together enough to fight. Sometimes I would say "No, I'm not," right out loud, often waking my husband with my loud, frightened retort.

Since it was obviously unfair for this nonsense to keep *both* of us awake, I got in the habit of stealing into the bathroom with my open Bible every time this happened. Getting back to sleep was impossible for an hour or two; so I used the time to memorize Scripture. I was using what Dick referred to in engineering as the displacement theory. Since our minds are created to entertain only one thought at a time, I reasoned that I could displace the tormenting, obsessive thoughts the enemy put into my mind with God's thoughts—Scripture. Gradually the torment would ease as fighting verses from the Word of God replaced the wrong thoughts of the destroyer. I came to understand what God means when He calls His Word the sword the Spirit wields. It is a weapon which is highly effective in warfare against a spiritual foe. We have to get to work and learn it, but it is the Spirit of God who wields it. Once we have a rich store, He will bring to mind just those passages which are appropriate for each particular round of the fight. Especially helpful to me during those nights were 2 Corinthians 10:3–5, Ephesians 6:10–18, Revelation 12:11, and Luke 10:19.

In time I came to see that the eternal verities of Scripture are our only absolute truths. All views contrary to them are lies, no matter how attractive they are, and ultimately come from a satanic source. Jesus said, "Whenever he speaks a lie, he speaks from his own nature; for he is a liar, and the father of lies." Jesus also said, "I am the way, and *the truth,* and the life; no one comes to the Father, but through me."

The great battle of life began to come into clear focus: in every area of thought and action we are to reject the diabolical lie or doubt and replace it with God's truth. It is just that simple, but those who learn this lesson will master every situation of life. Eve's problem was that she reversed the process: she rejected God's truth in favor of Satan's doubts and lies. Her progeny has been suffering from this perverseness ever since.

As the autumn of 1968 wore on and the riot of October color was followed by the bleak barrenness of November, my own soul struggled against bleak winter cold again. Oh, the teaching was going well all right (the tract had been laid aside; I just couldn't seem to get anywhere with that); but something was very, very wrong. Had I not proved I believed in the authority of the believer and moved out into the forefront of the battle? Why then my own apparent defeat? In my inner spirit I knew the reason why. I had not reckoned on the power of the fifth column still within.

Some nights, in addition to the verbal attacks against me, there would be a rattling sound in my throat, entirely divorced from any action on my part. Ruefully I began to face some facts I had been avoiding. Why had I been so tense after my deliverance in 1966? Was it possible that there were a whole group of other demons which had been stirred up but not cast out? Why had such terrible depression seized me soon after the lying spirit of prophecy was cast out? What other sinister forces lurked within my personality?

My moment of truth came when I had to face some stark facts about my behavior. About two weeks before Christmas that year, an incident occurred which let me and my family know that there were times when I could still lose complete control of myself.

Dick brought home a lovely Christmas tree one evening, which delighted the children. In those days I still managed the money in our home, and things had been close to the margin with us for some time. I asked him what he paid for it. He told me sheepishly. It was far more than we had ever paid for such a tree before.

Suddenly I flew into a violent rage from which I could find no escape. I shrieked and screamed at him, my voice rising in a geyser-like explosion of fury. My anger was a mad bronco, kicking and storming through the arena of our living room with my own personality a helpless rider, watching the spectacle yet powerless to do anything to stop it. Eventually it pitched me into an exhausted heap on the couch, where I lay moaning and groaning in contrition, begging forgiveness. The children were terrified.

Mutely Dick went out and exchanged the tree for a less expensive one to placate me. Every time I looked at it during that holiday, it pointed an accusing finger at me. There it stood, a stern reminder for all its tinseled glitter that I had lost complete control of myself the night we got it.

In desperation I phoned Maxwell Whyte, a minister with a big deliverance ministry in Scarborough, Ontario. With great kindness he urged me to come up to see them. Shortly before New Year's, Dick and I drove up to Canada for the weekend. We fought blinding snow most of the way and even had a minor accident, but God was with us. We arrived in the white-blanketed wonderland Saturday night, to find Pastor Whyte shoveling out a foot or more of snow from his own driveway. (This was quite a testimony to the power of the Lord, who had healed him of bronchial pneumonia not long before.)

The next morning after the church service, the pastor and Mrs. Whyte took us down to their prayer room in the basement. There they went to battle against the enemy in the most agressive way I had ever seen. They and their son and daughter-in-law all pled the blood of Jesus at once, and the pastor often commanded whatever demons were troubling me to leave me, loose me, and let me go.

Disappointingly, I did not have any clear manifestation of deliverance as I had with the sobbing in 1966. However, Mrs. Whyte shared with me her own deliverance from a spirit of fear which had plagued her in nocturnal attacks similar to my own experience. She said the time of commanding and battle had brought no apparent results either; yet afterward she was free from fear!

This was just the word I needed, and Maxwell Whyte himself gave me wise counsel which I was never to forget. He read Luke 10:19 to me, "Behold, I have given you authority to tread upon serpents and scorpions, and over all the power of the enemy, and nothing shall injure you."

"Do you believe that?" he asked me matter-of-factly.

"Why, of course I believe it," I answered, not very convincingly.

"Then start stomping, girl! Why, you are in the most vulnerable position possible, teaching others about the conflict and warning them of Satan's wiles while you carefully avoid *using* your authority yourself. No wonder they have been making mincemeat of you. Tell them to go—cast them out yourself whenever they bother you at all. You don't have to keep running up to Toronto again and again."

I knew he was right. I had taken the offensive in the teaching, but not in the application of the teaching. Our own Pastor Webber had said for years that when we do that, we are guilty of dead orthodoxy. For my clever self-deception I had paid a heavy price in counterattacks from enemy forces.

After we got home from Scarborough, I realized I was free from fear. I slept like a baby again, being awakened only once in a great while by a strange sensation or verbal attack. Even when such things did happen though, they did not frighten me as they had before. I would just calmly affirm my faith in Christ and the sufficiency of His blood sacrifice, quote a few relevant scriptures, and go back to sleep.

The day after we got home, I sat right down at my typewriter and wrote the tract on the occult. Now there were no hindrances, no sick and sleepy feelings, and my mind was completely clear for the task. I sent it off to the friend who worked for the tract publisher with a carefree heart.

Much to my amazement, that society never did publish it. They had a policy that the board must unanimously approve the publication of every manuscript, and there were twelve men on their board!

I forgot about the whole thing at that point. Dick accepted a job in upstate New York that June of 1969, and we left our many ties in New Jersey in another heart-wrenching move. My copy of the "Occult Experimentation" manuscript got lost in the process of relocating.

We were delighted with our new area, for it has a fine Christian day school where we send our younger children. At the first Parent-Teacher Fellowship meeting of the Loudonville Christian School, God brought me face to face with the man who was to publish the article on the occult. Dr. John Blanchard, the director of the National Association of Christian Schools, was speaker for the evening. His message revealed considerable insight into spiritual conflict.

In the coffee time and discussion following the message, I casually mentioned to him the fate of my manuscript warning against the occult. To my amazement, Dr. Blanchard told me he was the editor of *The Christian Teacher* and asked me to send him the article. I told him I had lost my copy, but that it had gotten to the galley proof stage with the tract publisher. Perhaps they would send it to him.

Some months later, having worked over the forwarded manuscript, he sent it to me for revision, conveying his suggestions for change and expansion accurately and simply. This encouragement was the primary incentive God used to launch me on my writing career. I was asked to write other things and sometimes felt an urge to get ideas down on paper.

Even before the occult article was published, new avenues were opening to me. At one time most of my speaking engagements had been as a returned missionary. Now most groups wanted to hear what I had learned about the spiritual conflict, especially the warning on occult involvement.

Soon I discovered that there was a real problem with this type of speaking engagement. Inevitably one or more of those present would be so agitated by the teaching that they would become either very emotional or openly antagonistic to me and to whomever had arranged for the meeting. There was clearly a need for deliverance in these cases, as far as I could determine. How was I to handle this?

Sometimes I would make it clear how to reach me later. Occasionally someone would do so. Oftener I would stay behind for special counseling. This usually worked out fairly well because only one or two would reveal a problem. My approach in counseling was to have the person confess all occult sins, break the demonic heredity, and tell Satan to go in the name of Jesus.

We had learned how to break the demonic heredity with a dramatic instance in our own family. A friend was visiting us who understood spiritual warfare, and we told him about the strange nightmares our youngest son was having. Just at three A.M. every morning, Billy would cry out in great terror for several minutes. Dick and I prayed over him at these times, commanding the spirit to depart and pleading the blood of Jesus. However, it always happened again the next night. Our friend told us it was the result of occult bondage somewhere in the family line that could be broken simply by speaking a command to that effect. He led us in a simple statement while Billy was upstairs in his bed asleep. The three A.M. nightmare pattern was broken. It never happened again.

With the publication of Hobart Freeman's book *Angels of Light* (a fine contemporary work on deliverance from occult oppression) we learned more about how to phrase such a statement. I would ask the person coming for counseling to say after me, "I now break, in the name of Jesus, all psychic heredity and any demonic hold upon my family line as a result of the disobedience of any of my ancestors." Reports of other nightmare patterns broken as a result of this procedure was encouraging.

One night I found myself beyond my depth, however. It was the week of winter recess for the children in February of 1970. I had taken the four of them to visit my folks near Easton, Maryland. A highlight of a visit in that area is Friday night prayer meeting at the home of an outstanding Christian opthamologist, Dr. Vince Earickson. Vince knew I was in town and called to ask me to speak on the occult at the Friday night meeting.

As soon as we came to the question period, I realized this group was different than the ones I usually addressed. Here there was an openness and liberty in the Spirit lacking in most places. These people did not have trouble being frank about their problems! I became very uneasy when Vince announced that I would be glad to counsel any who wanted help.

Fourteen people were waiting for me in the prayer room. My heart sank. I knew how to counsel one at a time, two or three could wait for one another, but what was I to do with fourteen?

It still makes me wince to remember how I botched the thing. I took out one at a time, using the procedure I have just described. At midnight several people remained in the prayer room; I had dealt with only three privately, and the rest had given up and gone home. Suddenly it struck me that the Lord Jesus never took people aside to command spirits to leave, but worked out in the open as he did when he healed the sick and taught them. Why did I have this notion that everything had to be so secretive anyway? As I thought about it, I became convinced I had been duped by Satan. Darkness and secrecy are usually *his* idea; God works in the light.

I suggested everyone confess his own sins, not minding the noise his neighbor made. Then I had them renounce the psychic heredity together; and everyone told Satan to leave, at once!

It was a noisy, rolicking business, but we all seemed to leave in a happy frame of mind. On the way home though, I had a frustrated, unfinished feeling. What if there were still specific demons in those people, not yet cast out? Had I just stirred up a hornet's nest, rather than getting rid of the hornets?

On the way back north next day, I poured out my complaint to God. "Lord, if You want me doing this sort of thing, You will have to teach me, that's all. You know how hard it is for me to know what to do about getting the demons out of *one* person, let alone a group. Please send some help before You ever let me get into a position like that again!"

Two weeks later that prayer was answered.

9
God's Answer

If I were asked to choose a day that stands out as the greatest milestone in this adventure with God, March 5, 1970 would be the day. Even remembering, I feel like a small child stealing down the staircase Christmas morning to find the shiny bike that eclipses his wildest dreams.

Snowy and blowy, the day arrived in the plain wrapper of typical upstate March weather; yet I knew it heralded a new era in my life, both from the quiet, this-is-it anticipation inside and from a sense of happy accomplishment. I had mailed my manuscript on the occult to John Blanchard that morning.

All day long as I busied myself with many of the common chores of housewifery, the glad sense of expectancy mounted. That evening we were scheduled to go to a meeting to hear charismatic author Don Basham. His book *Face Up With A Miracle* had been given to us a year before by close friends in California. I had read it through hungrily three or four times. It surprised me a great deal, not only because it spoke of miracles of healing and of praying in unknown

79

languages in our present day, but because it had been given to us by a couple who were once staunchly convinced that these things could not possibly be of God. Jody and Fred Stringer walked just about as close to the Lord as any people we knew; if *they* agreed with this fellow, we'd certainly have to give him a hearing.

At eight o'clock I clung to Dick's arm as my heels slid on the icy path leading to the wing of the Lutheran Church where the meeting was to be held. The snow had not amounted to enough for boots, but it was rough going without them. By March in our part of the country, everyone is rebelliously sick of winter. We tend to use any excuse to pretend it is nearly over, even though we can be fairly sure some of our worst storms still lie ahead. Ruefully I noted that we were to be in the basement, and I buttoned the wool bulky knit sweater I had on as soon as we took our seats.

Why in the world are we in the basement? I wondered. *I'll just freeze here tonight, I know it. What on earth are we doing in a Lutheran Church? Why, I wouldn't be caught dead in a liturgical church since my conversion. I wonder what this "full gospel" group is like anyway? I certainly hope we haven't made a mistake coming here and bringing friends.*

"Pat, which one of these fellows is the speaker, do you know?" Jim's voice next to me broke my reverie. He and his wife had come with us.

"I have no idea, Jim," I said as a slumping, gray-haired hulk of a man in a blue sport jacket shifted in the seat just in front of me. "I don't even know who the president of the Full Gospel Business Men's Fellowship is. We have never attended any of their meetings."

At that point the singing began, ending our conversation. The president then introduced Don Basham, and the husky form in the blue sport jacket rose to his feet. The first thing I noticed about him was a certain recklessness in the way he dressed, not at all the suited, white-shirted, proper type of individual I had come to associate with the ministry. The second thing was a freedom and casualness in him which would have seemed inappropriate in a religious setting had it not been so disarming. The third thing which registered about this surprising man was a steadying calm and sureness about him, emphasized by his low-voiced, rather rapid-fire Texas drawl.

He did not fit my imaginary portrait of an Elijah. He did not boom at us with stern pronouncements or apocryphal threats. Yet before this night was over, we would find out that he could call down fire from heaven.

My face broke into a wide grin as he announced his topic for the evening—deliverance from evil spirits. He introduced the subject as part of the fourfold ministry of Jesus: Savior, Healer, Deliverer, and Baptizer in the Holy Spirit. During the hour-long message and further hour of questions and answers, I learned more than I had in the five or six years previous. It was like a graduate course on the subject.

Don Basham obviously did not stay in one place very long. It was evident from his allusions to travel that he had taught all over North America, in Europe on both sides of the Iron Curtain, as well as in New Zealand and other remote places. In fact constant travel was the outstanding characteristic of his ministry.

At the end of the question period, Basham stopped for a moment, gazing out over the group, apparently trying to decide whether he was actually finished or not.

"Well, how about it?" he asked, scratching the back of his head. "We can pause a minute, and if some of you feel you have to leave, you can. Those of you who want to stick it out, can go through these prayers. Do any of you here feel, after what you've heard, that you can be helped by a ministry of deliverance? Do you want to check yourself out to see if some of the problems you've been struggling with are because of tormenting spirits? Let's see a show of hands of those who would like to stay."

About fifty hands went up. Since there were approximately a hundred present, this was quite a positive response. I was amazed that so many church people could be so honest about their need.

"Well, praise the Lord," Don commented matter-of-factly. "Now, let me lead you in this prayer of renunciation of the occult:

"Dear Lord Jesus Christ," we all repeated after him. "I have a confession to make. I have sought supernatural experience apart from you; I have dabbled in psychic things, and by this I have opened my personality to the psychic realm, and disobeyed your Word. I'm sorry, Lord, and I want you to forgive me. Help me renounce these things and close my personality to this realm.

"In Jesus' name I renounce hypnotism and ouija boards, spiritualism and reincarnation. I renounce ESP, palm reading, astrology and horoscopes. In the name of Jesus Christ I renounce everything psychic or occult and all witchcraft and sorcery. I renounce every cult that denies the blood of Christ, every philosophy that denies the divinity of Christ. In Jesus' name I renounce all these things and call upon the Lord to set me free. Amen.

"Now we'll do the same thing about forgiveness. When we say, in Jesus' name I forgive . . ., you put names in there. If husband and wife are here, and one of you holds resentment against the other say the name. Don't hold anything back. This is very important. Okay, let's repeat this one:

"Dear Lord Jesus," we all began with him again, "I have another confession to make. I've hated certain people, had bitterness and resentment, and I'm sorry, Lord. I will to forgive them; I want your help.

"In Jesus' name I forgive . . . (Speak the name out loud—John, Joe, Mary, Father, Mother, Grandfather, wife, husband, children.)

"Lord Jesus, you bring the names to mind.

"Speak the names out loud, not real loud, but speak them out. Don't hold any name back. If there's some person you feel a little huffy about, a little bitter toward, that's someone you ought to mention.

"Thank you, Lord. Thank you, Jesus. Thank you, Lord.

"Now in case you haven't remembered someone, say, in Jesus' name I forgive everyone I've hated and resented. I ask you to forgive me as I have forgiven them. In Jesus' name I forgive myself. Amen

"I'm a child of God saved by the grace of Jesus Christ. I know He died on the cross for me; I know He shed His blood for my sins, and He's my Lord and my Savior. I've committed my life to Him, and I hereby renounce all of the works of Satan. I renounce every evil spirit that binds or torments me. In the name of Jesus Christ I renounce them all and call upon the Lord to set me free. In Jesus' name, Amen.

"In just a minute I'm going to take authority over any spirit bothering anybody; so let me give you a word of advice before we start. Nothing may happen—we may not stir up anything—but we usually do, and sometimes it gets a little bizarre. Somebody may cry or moan; someone may let out a shriek, or somebody may yell or fall on the floor. I don't particularly expect these things to happen, but sometimes they do and I want to let you know ahead of time. Don't be surprised. The devil is a show-off, and he's trying to frighten you. I've seen about everything; so you watch me. If I don't get scared, you don't get scared. If I get scared, we'll shut the whole thing down."

Whatever he said after that was lost in the gale of laughter that went through the room—a startling contrast between this joyful, liberated approach and the fears most people have about opposing Satan.

"Did someone bring a roll of paper towels? Good. Let's keep it handy. Sometimes when we get into this, there is quite a bit of coughing and gagging. Then it's nice to have them handy. This is not a dignified ministry: the devil's not a very dignified fellow. He likes to frighten people. Even when Jesus ministered, it wasn't a quiet, reverent thing. The spirits cried out with a loud voice, and sometimes threw people down. Don't worry if this happens. It may not; everybody may be real respectable. You may just sigh or burp them out.

"Now, to take authority over these things, I'm going to start a verbal attack against the spirits in everybody here.

When I do, I want you, if you know what it is, to renounce it in your own mind and command it to come out of you in the name of Jesus, as I'm going to be doing. If you feel something begin to shake up inside you, and you have to cough or sigh or cry to get it out, or weep or moan or whatever, you do it. I'll watch to see if somebody is particularly distressed or shaky. Some of you may already feel a little shaky, queasy in the stomach, nervous. This is a good sign. Things are kicking up, and you're going to get rid of them. I'll come over to help you out and command the thing to identify itself. But you don't have to wait for me. You can get your own deliverance. Then you may turn, if somebody beside you is having trouble, and help them out.

"Now let's pray a prayer of protection and turn it all over to the Lord.

"Lord Jesus, we thank you that in your death on the cross you defeated Satan and all of his evil spirits. Thank you, Lord, for deliverance. We look to you now and plead the precious protection of your blood over us as we get into this. You are the Deliverer; we are only instruments in your hands. Protect us all. Protect my family in Florida, Lord. Protect this church and all the families here by your precious shed blood. Thank you, Lord, for victory in your name. Amen.

"All right, Satan, you hear me. I come against you and every evil spirit binding anyone in this room. You spirits know who I am, a servant of the most high God, and I take authority over every one of you in the name of Jesus Christ. I command you to manifest yourselves. I plead the blood of Christ against you. You will not remain hidden or silent; you will come to the surface and come out of the people of God. Hallelujah. Thank you, Lord.

"Take it easy now, folks, and see what we get into. The blood. The blood. Satan, you have to yield. You know you are a defeated foe. You know you cannot resist the name of Jesus Christ. In the name of Jesus I take authority over every spirit in every person. Thank you, Lord. Hallelujah. Praise you, Jesus.

"Anybody here feeling real shaky or queasy inside? Okay, praise the Lord. Where are the paper towels?"

Don walked over to a woman sitting right behind me who was apparently feeling very upset. "Do you know what started this? Well, we're going to find out. Spirit, you're subject to me in the name of Jesus. I command you to give me your name."

"Oh, I'm so confused," she moaned.

"There is a spirit of *confusion*. Renounce this spirit in Jesus' name."

"I renounce the spirit of *confusion* in Jesus' name," the woman said weakly with obvious effort.

"Okay, spirit of *confusion*, come out of her in Jesus' name."

Almost immediately there was a series of quick, harsh coughs from the woman, who then began to tremble again. Don took authority over the spirit *epilepsy*. Two others were cast out of her in rapid succession, but by that time agitation in the back of the room caused him to move on.

The woman began to moan, and a terrific battle began in my own mind. She apparently really needed help. I knew how. Should I just sit and play it safe, or should I cast that demon out of her—while at least ten or twelve members of our church watched?

It was not a small matter. The decision I made in those few seconds could prove an irrevocable step in my life. Dick had moved to the back of the room, and I could not get his opinion. Seldom have I felt so alone with God or has an issue been so plain: was I going to please God or man? Could I risk the displeasure and gossip which might follow, or not?

"Lord," I prayed, "if I'm not doing the right thing, have the speaker discourage me."

I stood up and turned around, "Demon now manifesting, what is your name?"

The spirits named themselves quickly and came out on the first command. They were getting in the habit of leaving!

"Say, praise the Lord for the help," Don said as he walked by. "You keep right at it. There's a lot of work here tonight."

On the other side of the room, my close friend, Eleanore

Smith, was having her own inner battle. Acute anxiety had surfaced as soon as the speaker took authority over the spirits. She knew she needed help. Could she afford to let this opportunity slip by, even though she might be rejected by those who looked on her as a spiritual leader in the community?

Four years after she and Carl returned from Cameroun, Eleanore had been hurled from her bed to the floor by a violent convulsion. During a ten-day hospital stay and exhaustive tests, nothing more conclusive than some disturbance in her brain wave pattern was discovered. She was placed on medication, but no medical help could restore her power to remember.

For five long years Eleanore could get nothing from her personal study of the Bible. She had to give up teaching Bible studies and Bible clubs for children, for she could not even remember when she prepared just beforehand with notes. This was an excruciating trial, since she and her husband had been missionaries for over a decade, and her whole life had revolved around sharing the Lord and His Word with others.

Eleanore looked around the room. Beyond the confusion of coughs, gags, and moans, it was evident that sinister powers, long hidden, were being forced to expose themselves and yield to the mighty power of God. As she watched one man retching violently and spitting phlegm into a paper towel, she realized this group could not be accused of playing church.

Wistfully Eleanore thought of a testimony Basham had shared at the end of his message. A woman bound by an occult spirit had been unable to read or understand her Bible for years. Now after her deliverance, she was free and loved the Word again. Eleanore made her decision; this possibility was too thrilling to miss from fear of making a fool of herself. Her hand shot up.

Don came against the first spirit troubling her; it was *forgetfulness*. Eleanore renounced it two or three times in the name of Jesus. As soon as he gave the command, she coughed and an overpowering odor of sulphur filled the room.

"I guess that's hardly surprising, considering where these things hale from," Don commented.

"There's something else," Eleanore said. "I can feel something sticking in my throat."

"What's your name, demon?" Don demanded.

As the word *self-pity* came to mind, Eleanore flinched in disbelief.

"Self-pity? Why, I never would have dreamed I had that one!"

"Let's renounce it," Don said matter-of-factly. "It's one of the commonest of the evil spirits."

When this one was commanded out, she let out a deep sigh; then joy came—deep, powerful waves of liberty and a sense of the Lord's closeness.

At this point I looked over from the other side of the room. To my amazement Eleanore's face was bathed in a radiance I had not seen since we first met in 1958, on one of their furloughs. After this brief but spectacular deliverance, it was evident that the glad spontaneity was back.

Gratitude to God filled my soul, and for the first time in my life both my hands went up in an unplanned expression of praise to our wonderful Lord. I saw a few shocked faces nearby and had to grin. It really was no way for a well-taught fundamentalist to behave out in public. Suddenly I realized, without a trace of regret or embarrassment, that the Lord had liberated me from the last moorings of fear of man. It no longer made any difference what others thought of me if only Jesus were pleased. Glory filled my soul in that moment of freedom.

Before long it was all over. The last few people were getting ready to go, and Dick was holding my coat. All evening a burning desire had been growing in me to experience all that God had for me. For years I had shunned the idea that I needed the gifts in the Spirit in order to be the person I longed to be, but in one evening of watching God work through this servant of His, my last argument died. Suddenly I decided that I would not let Don Basham leave without praying for me. I wanted all that he had of the Holy Spirit.

"Have you ever spoken in tongues?" Don asked me.

"No, I never even wanted to," I admitted. "I did ask the Lord for the power of the Holy Spirit in my life back in 1959. After that there was a change, because people started coming to the Lord through my witness."

"Great!" Don said, as he steered me to a nearby chair. "Now come into your full inheritance. As I lay hands on you and pray, God will give you words of praise in a new language. You won't understand them, and there will probably just be a few syllables. They might flit through your mind, or you might see them as you close your eyes—something like on a teletype machine."

"What if I get a phony gift from that tricker?" I whispered, verbalizing the awful doubt that crossed my mind as the devil made a last frantic attempt to keep me from life in the Spirit.

"Shame on you!" Don said sternly. "The Word says, 'What man is there among you, when his son shall ask him for a loaf, will give him a stone? Of if he shall ask for a fish, he will not give him a snake, will he?' Here you are in the deliverance ministry yourself, and you are doubting that God will give you the fullness of the Holy Spirit if you ask Him!"

The attack hit home. I saw how unreasonable and foolish I had been about speaking in tongues.

"Remember, no English," Don instructed me. "Just say the words that are there. *You* have to say them, just as *they* did in Acts 2:4. The miracle is the provision of the language, but you still have to do the speaking."

I closed my eyes, and Don prayed for me, quietly and with great fluency, in a language he had never learned. It was definitely not gibberish; it had vocabulary and sentence structure.

Then I saw in my mind's eye a few strange syllables spelled phonetically, *me li te fy o me.* I said them out loud. No strange power came over me and said them for me. I used my own voice and spoke in exactly the same tone I use for speaking English, but the Holy Spirit provided the words. That's all there was to it.

This calm, unemotional experience was a far cry from the overwhelming fervor I had expected.

"I guess I'm just too fluent in English ever to be very good at that."

"Never mind. More will come later," Don insisted as he walked away to pick up his own things and get ready to go. "Praise the Lord; that was it."

By the time Dick and I had gotten to the car, I had begun to doubt the whole experience. It was nothing like I had expected and dreaded all these years. Probably what I had believed and taught for so long was true after all: since we all receive the Holy Spirit when we are born again, it simply did not matter whether a believer spoke in tongues or not.

Or did it?

All the way home I was aware of an amazing feeling from deep within, a great welling up of love. I felt I could reach out and hug the whole world. Wave upon wave of glory seemed to spring up from some source deep inside.

Two scripture verses flashed across my mind. "He who believes in Me, as the Scripture said, 'From his innermost being shall flow rivers of living water.'" "These signs will accompany those who have believed: in My name they will cast out demons, they will speak with new tongues."

How strange it was that I had accepted the Word of God as my final authority, while believing one half of Mark 16:17 and rejecting the other half. Perhaps stranger was the rationalization that the little trickle of love in my life could possibly be a full expression of the inexhaustible fountain of God's infinite love. For years I had *tried* to love people for Jesus' sake; in the days that followed, I was to find that love was an effortless spilling over from a deep inner reservoir.

Calvary love. In rivers. Rivers of living water.

10
A Few Housewives—and the Holy Spirit

For people who believe in luck, it might seem the day we picked, Friday the thirteenth of March, was a poor choice for our first group deliverance meeting without a visiting expert. However, we found demon powers were just as frightened as they had been the week before at the church basement meeting.

The day before I had taught our Thursday ladies' Bible study as usual. The lesson was a summary of Scripture warnings against the occult, and several newcomers came. One of them, Stella, seemed to be a very troubled girl. She sat on the edge of her seat for the whole hour, moving her feet ceaselessly back and forth in front of her. There was a restless, tormented expression on her face and a settled look of unhappiness about her eyes.

I felt fairly sure God wanted me to take a public stand against the powers of evil and hold the same kind of unashamed, public group session we had seen the week before. To test my hunch, I asked if there were those who would like to come to a deliverance meeting the following morning. Several hands went up, Stella's among them.

As Friday dawned I woke up with a sense of expectancy. I still felt the anointing, almost overpowering feeling of love, but there were a few questions in my mind. What if the mighty power were gone, since we had no veteran man of God present? What if the spirits refused to name themselves when I commanded them to do so? What if nothing happened when I took authority over the spirits? This thought made me very uncomfortable!

I need not have worried. Eleven miles away in Scotia, the Lord was taking care of the situation beautifully. My dear friend Eleanore Smith was in the bathtub praying for the meeting. She mentioned everything she could think of, then decided to pray the few syllables in her prayer language which she had received in California months before when baptized in the Holy Spirit. Suddenly right there in the bathtub, the windows of heaven opened, and Eleanore burst into a flow of fluent, rich vocabulary in the unknown tongue. Later that morning we were to see the results such prayer in the Spirit can bring.

At ten o'clock several cars were already parked in our driveway. I had been hustling around doing dishes, making beds, and sweeping the kitchen floor. There had been very little time for prayer, but I had been fasting. In fact all the girls who came had gone without breakfast. We were making a definite attempt to prepare ourselves spiritually for whatever God wanted.

As we all gathered in the family room, I was amazed to see eleven of us. Eleanore and I had wondered whether shame would keep most of the girls away. However, we found that when the real needs of real people are being met, false pride and hypocritical masks are about as popular as a three-cent stamp.

Stella was there, shifting her feet back and forth in front of her as she had on Thursday. From the time she came in, she kept up a nervous chatter in rapid, machine gun fire rhetoric, even on the intake of breath.

Just before we got started, Dora came. She had just undergone a series of medical tests to find out the cause of recent fainting and dizzy spells. Her doctors had found no answer for her, but since she had blacked out completely a few times, she was forbidden to drive. When I loaned her *Angels of Light,* Dora had seen her first ray of hope in a seemingly bleak situation. She had confessed all instances of occult dabbling to God and told Satan to leave her in Jesus' name. Although she noticed some relief after this, the dizzy spells persisted. She suspected she was still far from free and finally got the courage to come to our meeting.

At ten-fifteen I prayed God would protect and guide us, covering each family represented by the blood of Jesus Christ. After that we renounced the occult sins and prayed prayers of forgiveness. This whole process was not at all professional. We had to keep reminding each other of things Don Basham had led us in renouncing, and we certainly did not remember everything.

Then the big moment to take authority over the demons present came. I had never done this before. Until last week's meeting I had only addressed Satan and then named what I *guessed* to be the problem in the troubled person. I had never commanded the evil spirits to name themselves.

"Okay," I said, clearing my throat, "let's get down to business. I take authority over you, Satan, and over all demons troubling anyone here, as a blood-bought child of God. In the name of the Lord Jesus Christ, I command you to come to the surface and identify yourselves. Give us your name, each one, and then you are going to come out."

The whole room seemed electric with power, but for several minutes nothing happened. We began to sing that wonderful old chorus, "There's Power in the Blood." Then I remembered a strange thing that Don Basham had done right after he took authority over the spirits. He had walked back and forth saying, "Praise Jesus. Thank you, Lord," even before anything had happened!

"Praise Jesus," I said self-consciously, feeling a little odd. "Thank you, Lord. Say, why don't we all get our hands up and get rid of our spiritual bursitis? It's in the Bible to raise your hands. I don't know why we never do it."

In that minute or two each of us threw off our restraint, praising Jesus with our hands up in the air. Grinning at each other in this rather novel experience, we all noticed something we were to comment on later. It felt *good!*

Then the action began.

Suddenly my close friend and neighbor, Beverly Strott, began to shake and sob violently. I walked over to the couch where she was sitting and spoke directly to the spirit troubling her.

"Demon now manifesting, give us your name."

There was no answer, but the sobbing and shaking became more pronounced. All at once three girls in the room got the word *pride* imprinted on their minds. We reasoned that this must be the gift of discerning spirits mentioned in 1 Corinthians 12. God had certainly confirmed the name by giving it to more than one.

"Why don't you renounce it that way, Beverly?" I asked. "Just say, 'I renounce the spirit of *pride* in the name of Jesus.'"

With great difficulty Beverly got the words out. The sobbing increased for a moment or so before it ceased altogether. Then she sat bolt upright, wiping her eyes and beginning to grin.

"Say, I feel just great," she said. "That wasn't bad at all."

We all laughed and had a couple minutes to talk about this experience before another demon began to act up across the room. Stella was vigorously shaking her head from side to side in rapid, negative motions.

The command to this demon to identify itself made it talkative, a phenomenon I have seen many times since.

"He touched me!" Stella announced triumphantly, with a haughty expression on her face. "He touched me right on the shoulder."

"Who touched you?" I asked.

"The Lord," she said in a patronizing way, "as He often does."

"Nonsense!" I snorted. "The Lord doesn't physically touch people today. You are deceived. That thing has you thinking you are something special by this delusion."

Stella's hands went to her head, and her face showed excruciating pain. "Ooooooh, my head," she moaned. "You've hurt my *pride!*"

"That's it," someone said, "a spirit of *pride* like the one that just left Beverly."

The contortions of Stella's face and the sudden resumption of the insistent head shaking left us in no doubt that we had hit the mark. Stella renounced it, but it did not come out easily. We commanded and sang "There's Power in the Blood" for several minutes; however, I had to quote several scripture verses on pride before the thing would turn loose.

When the demon left her, Stella's body started up from the couch as if she were planning to stand up. Her face and body wrenched in pain as the harsh, rasping cough began which signaled her release from the bondage of this other personality.

"Wow! That thing almost took the front of my head with it," she said in amazement. "To think some people doubt there are such things as demons!"

For about two minutes Stella had peace. Then she began sobbing uncontrollably in the same falsetto way Beverly had. Again the Lord was faithful and gave Eleanore its name, *self-pity*. This one came out much more quickly. However after it left, Stella slipped to the floor as if completely exhausted.

She was not unconscious. In fact she sat up and started to laugh, hideous laughter, not at all expressive of joy—an unreasoning, idiotic giggle, utterly inappropriate for the situation.

We demanded the name of this spirit, but got no answer. No one had any idea what it might be. I decided to guess. "It seems like a silly, teasing spirit to me," I said.

On command the laughing stopped, but there was no cough nor change in Stella's facial expression. In fact, I realized ruefully, there was no real indication that the demon had left.

Suddenly Dora began to talk rather strangely from the big

wing chair next to the fireplace. She started reminiscing about some of the problems in her family and had a strange, faraway look in her eyes. I came over to her and commanded the spirit to give us its name. She kept right on talking, but her conversation began to contain the word *epilepsy* very frequently. She mentioned one or another member of her family who had been afflicted with this disease, expressing fear that she was becoming ill.

Basham had taught us that some of the spirits confess themselves through conversation. He mentioned that if we listen carefully, we shall hear the name of the demon or the type of the torment it represents being repeated over and over again as the troubled person speaks.

"I think it's the spirit of *epilepsy,* Dora," I said. "Renounce it in the name of Jesus."

"I renounce—the—spirit—of—*epilepsy*—in Jesus' name," Dora whispered. It apparently took all the strength she could muster to say these few words.

As soon as I began to command that demon to leave her, an amazing thing happened. Dora's face twisted and contorted in a sub-human way, as if an invisible pair of hands were wringing out the muscles and nerves just beneath the skin. Immediately the ghastly sallowness she had had all morning left her complexion, and it became pink and normal looking. For the first time since her arrival, Dora smiled.

She said in wonder, "I don't even remember what happened during these last few minutes. It's as if I blanked out."

"Do you feel any different?" someone asked.

"Oh, I feel *free,*" she said. "That heavy, hazy feeling has left my head, and I know I'll be able to drive again now."

Kindergarten children were coming home for lunch, and houses had to be cleaned for the weekend. Soon the door closed behind the last visitor. As I walked upstairs with the dry mop, I suddenly realized each step was taking me further and further away from the life I had known ever since my conversion. I had lived a life of appearances, trying to please people. As long as the outward circumstances looked all right, I had assumed I could get by. I had believed *in* God, but I had not *believed God* all those powerless years. Doubtless this was why the signs spoken of in Mark 16:17 and 18 had never followed me. That Friday morning I knew I could never again shut my eyes to any part of Scripture, either with clever doctrinal gymnastics or subtle rationalizations. I had left the realm of safe respectability behind when I spoke the first words of the unknown prayer language the week before.

Suddenly I realized that everything the Lord Jesus did in the first century, He wants to do now. The only thing which has ever stopped Him is the unbelief of His people. Having tasted His power, His freedom, and His victory, who could ever go back to a life of impotence?

Reaching the landing in my upstairs hall, I little dreamed what my new life in the Spirit would cost in terms of slander, opposition, and unpopularity. One thing I did know however: it didn't matter any more.

Late that night I tossed and turned in my bed. Dick had been asleep for over an hour, but I was so tense that I felt like an overwound clock. My body was as rigid as a rusted, corroded engine, and I was icy cold.

Twice I got up, once to put on some wool athletic socks and once to find some mittens. I had the electric blanket turned up to high, but was still freezing. My teeth chattered as I tried to pray under my breath.

"Lord, what's the matter?" I whispered, closing my eyes.

Suddenly the word *self-pity* was imprinted in bold, capital letters across my mind. So this was my problem! I had a demon which had been mightily bothered by the events of the morning, and since we had all renounced it and it had come out of two other people, it evidently knew its time was up in my life too.

My mind flashed back over my stormy adolescent years. I could almost see myself standing at a desolate graveside when I was sixteen years old, not knowing where to take my grief. "Someday my prince will come" had become "My prince came—and died."

A shudder went through me as I relived the weird, haunted nights with the eerie breathing so close to my ear. I remembered some of the hopeless thoughts of the months I spent as a classic insomniac. *What could I possibly do with my life, now that the light had gone out? How could I ever hope for happiness? Where could I run to hide from an existence stretching interminably before me? Who would understand me? Where was God, if indeed, there was a God?*

My ruthless memory took me on to my honeymoon on Cape Cod. We had just gone swimming in Provincetown, and I was sitting in the car, waiting for Dick to take a few pictures. As I looked at his tired, rather worried face, that same hopeless feeling swept over me again. *Why on earth did I marry him?* I had thought. *He can never make me happy. What made me do it? Did some strange force bring us together so we could be miserable all the time?*

The scenes rushed on in rapid succession before my mind's eye.

There was the absurd daydreaming about the words the psychiatrist had spoken so many years before: "Someday, you will meet someone who will not only be like the one you lost; it will be he."

There was the encounter with a certain someone who seemed so *familiar* to me. I winced as I remembered the long hours of pouring out our problems to each other, finding that we had so much in common. Just as Dick would never understand me, so his wife had built-in inadequacies that made it impossible for her ever to understand him. What empathy we had for one another, what amazing rapport and ability to communicate!

The merciless conveyor belt of unwelcome tableaus kept on running through my mind. First there was silly glance-stealing, then the absurd flirtation; finally there was the convenient move from the area which removed me from the scene of temptation—all that kept me from slipping into adultery. Deep down in my heart, I knew I was no better than those who were having full-fledged affairs. Didn't Jesus say, "Whoever looks . . . to lust . . . has committed adultery already . . . in his heart?"

"Why, I bet he had the same demon," I said right out loud. "No wonder there was that magnetic pull between us. Twin spirits, that's what they were. Okay, you spirit of *self-pity*. You've been found out. Now you get out in Jesus' name."

Suddenly a series of violent coughs came from somewhere inside me, racking my body and completely taking my breath away. I could not seem to stop for several minutes. Finally I lay still and limp. My body was now completely relaxed; every trace of tenseness had left with the demon.

No wonder I felt tense after my initial deliverance four years ago, I thought. *With that thing still in me, no wonder I had a lot of bad days. This one was apparently the big one, the boss. Praise Jesus for this glorious deliverance.*

Then I slept—soundly, peacefully, dreamlessly. It was my best night's sleep in twenty-three years.

The next morning brought the dawn of a new era. I looked out at the world through different eyes. From the moment I first glanced out the window as I put my slippers on, I noticed the change. The winter white on the lawn and trees was not dreary; it was a cheery, sentimental Christmas card scene, pointing up the coziness of our lovely, warm home.

Ham and pancakes were not a bore to make that Saturday morning. They were fun! It wasn't a drag to have them all home from work and school. It was an adventure—homely and routine, but exhilarating and a real joy nonetheless.

How has Dick put up with me all these years? I thought as I handed him his coffee. *Beth Ann is getting so pretty. Look at her clearing the orange juice glasses without being told. That Charlie, he's really a wit. I wonder why I never noticed these things before. Johnny —listen to him talk. He could hold his own on "Meet the Press." And Billy is following right in his footsteps. A lot of adults couldn't talk as sensibly about the return of Christ as that four year old.*

What a wonderful family we have, I mused, as the thoughts kept racing through my mind. *And to think, it took the unlikely combination of Dick and me to pair up these particular sets of chromosomes and genes. Maybe it hasn't been such a bad thing after all!*

11

"My Name Is Legion, for We Are Many"

A wave of nausea swept over Stella as she left our family room that Friday morning. Suddenly she remembered a similar experience a year ago when she had heard Maxwell Whyte speak on spiritual warfare. As she zipped up her boots and buttoned her coat, Stella felt the same seasick feeling she felt that night.

Whyte had invited those to stay who felt they might need deliverance. When he passed her chair, he laid his hands on her head and that awful churning began, but there was no relief.

Stella thought about this as she walked down our back stairs and got into her car. Why had she not received help a year ago? For a moment she fumbled for her keys in an overcrowded bag; then the truth hit her. During the Bible teaching the day before she had learned that forgiveness was essential preparation for being liberated. Without this, ridding her life of demons was as hard as trying to start her car without the ignition key.

Today as far as she knew, she had forgiven everyone—

even her mother. Stella's eyes filled at the thought of one who had never wanted her and had openly rejected her throughout her childhood. A year ago she still had a reservoir of resentment and reaction stored within her. No wonder she was not a candidate for deliverance then.

As she backed down our driveway and headed toward home, Stella thought of the parable of the unforgiving servant in Matthew 18. She remembered that his master had forgiven him a ten million dollar debt, then the servant turned around and refused to forgive his fellow servant a seventeen dollar debt.

Yes, the Bible was still relevant all right. Stella reasoned that Jesus had paid for all the rebellion and wrongdoing of a lifetime by the sacrifice of His own blood; yet she had been unwilling to forgive her mother. "And his lord, moved with anger, handed him over to the torturers until he should repay all that was owed him. 'So shall My heavenly Father also do to you, if each of you does not forgive his brother from your heart.' "

Stella did not have an easy time that weekend. All day Saturday she felt sick and full of anxiety at the thought of attending a company party with Sam, her husband. She felt she was getting resistance from a whole opposing army in the unseen realm. Finally, in desperation she said, "I *will* go. You leave me alone in the name of Jesus Christ," and the problem lifted. The party went smoothly.

Monday morning I was to speak to a group familiar to Stella at a prayer meeting in another area. I did not know where the place was, so Stella offered to take me. It was a wonderful opportunity. We had good fellowship on the trip down, and an interesting time after we got to the meeting.

I had been asked to teach on the occult. The same thing happened that I had noticed many times before. This subject cannot be denounced without reaction from the evil powers within some of the people present.

One girl, an obese mental patient with suicidal tendencies,

was extremely agitated by the teaching. She sobbed and wailed, disconcerting the rest of the group who were unable to comfort her in any way. I suggested that if the others agreed, we try to help her. There seemed to be a positive response, so I led them through renunciations of the occult and prayers of forgiveness. Then I took authority over the spirits.

The girl mentioned several things which were troubling her, but it was impossible to tell whether she was really being delivered or not. She did not cough, sigh, burp or scream, and she had a noticeable desire to maintain the pity and sympathy of the group. She did become somewhat more cheerful and positive however, and we all hoped that she had reached a turning point in her condition.

While I was trying to help her, Stella started that hideous, uncontrollable laughter again. When we got to a good stopping place with the stout girl, I walked over to Stella and commanded the laughing demon to name itself just as I had on Friday. There was still no response from her, but one of the other girls present spoke up.

"She started to laugh like that when you were dealing with the demon *madness* in Mary," she said.

"Thanks a lot," I said. "Okay, Stella, renounce the spirit of *madness* in Jesus' name."

With great difficulty Stella stammered and stumbled over the words.

"I re—re—re—renounce the sp—sp—sp—spirit of *madness* in Jesus' name," she stammered.

"Come out of her, spirit of *madness,* in the name of the Lord Jesus Christ," I said.

In the instant that the command was given, Stella's eyes closed and her hands reached upward in a tortuous, pleading gesture as great, writhing, snakelike motions slithered through her body. An earsplitting scream came from her lips as the demon which had caused so much difficulty in her life left her for good. Afterward her body went limp, her hands fell loosely at her sides and her head dropped to one side.

"Everything's churning around in there now," Stella said.

"There's a real earthquake going on inside me. That one seemed to rip me apart as it left me."

For the next hour Stella was so exhausted that she could hardly keep her head up and sit in the group of chatting ladies. Fortunately, the women had planned to have us for lunch, so she did not have to drive right away. By the time we were ready to go, she was able to make the trip.

On the way home Stella told me she felt more at peace, but she still felt quite tense.

"You know, Pat," she said, "I think I've got a lot of these demons. Do me a favor, will you? Let me know every time you go anywhere to minister deliverance. I've got a hunch cleaning me out is going to take a good, long time."

Stella proved to be an accurate prophet. In the year that followed she was delivered from many, many demons. Each time we noticed a greater liberty in her face and a greater calm in her whole demeanor. These evil spirits were apparently clustered in her personality in groups, and they had to be dealt with layer by layer. She found she could not rush the process. Once I asked her why she felt she (and others with large numbers of demons) needed to be liberated progressively, rather than all in one fell swoop.

"Because I couldn't stand it any more quickly," she told me. "The Lord is merciful, and He knows how much I can take at any one time. Then too, I have to stand against them after they've been cast out. It's unwise to try to stand against too many at once. In a way, it's like convalescence after a long illness. You regain your strength slowly, but steadily. As time goes on, you can take on more. The Lord warned that they would try to come back again.

"Sometimes it takes several weeks for me to learn the scripture to stand against a particularly powerful demon. When the temptation to slip back into the torment it caused comes again, I recognize that the demon is trying to come back. Then I have to get God's Word in there to fill the empty places the spirit formerly inhabited. I believe being saturated with appropriate scripture is the way the Holy Spirit can control areas given to the devil before."

One day Stella came to my home, shaking all over. From the time she walked into my kitchen until she left, she could not seem to stop coughing.

"Pat, you've just got to help me," she pled desperately. "There's a whole group just at the surface in me right now, and I can't seem to get at them myself. I've been casting them out without any outside help lately and have had pretty good success, but these that are bugging me right now just won't name themselves, and they won't let go."

"Well," I suggested, "there's a meeting early next week over in Schenectady; how about that?"

"I can't wait that long," she said in a fresh fit of coughing. "I need help right now, or I think I'll cough to death."

It was obvious that something had to be done. "Okay," I said, "let's plan it for tonight. Jenny wants a meeting over at her house, because it is hard for her to get out. Why don't we call to see if she can have it tonight?"

That evening was an unforgettable experience. I had never learned or seen more that has helped me to help other people.

In the weeks preceding this meeting, all the demons that had been coming out of Stella were in the realm of attitudes. Stella, herself, noticed this and related it to teaching we had received from our pastor. He pointed out that we are made of spirit, soul, and body. He recommended a book, *The Release of the Spirit* by Watchman Nee, in which Nee postulates that a man ordinarily lives by the dictates of his soul and body; however, God wants us to live under the control of the Holy Spirit who only dwells in the spirit of the believer. No demon can touch this area in a Christian, but it can be so obscured by our soulish desires and physical needs that we are almost unaware of its existence.

That night the first demon to name itself was the demon *affliction,* which ushered in a dramatic new era of deliverance for *Stella,* who had had the demon *Legion* cast out of her a few weeks before. We knew that we were dealing with many demons, but now we found we had moved from the soulish into the physical realm. At first we found that the afflictive demon would not respond to commands to come out.

This was another of those wonderful times when we all realized the Lord Jesus Christ is the true head of these deliverance meetings. Not only is He the sole deliverer, but He is the only source of wisdom and strength. There is profound truth in His words, "apart from Me you can do nothing."

God gave us a firm conviction that Stella should talk out her problems, which proved to be the word of wisdom which unlocked her bondage. She began to pour out a description of scarring emotional experiences in her childhood and in her marriage. The catharsis liberated her psychologically, removing the ground on which the afflictive demon had preyed.

Tears flowed freely. Once Stella was calm and talked out, we went after the demon again. It came out easily now, followed by the spirit of *nervousness*. At its expulsion, Stella's head wrenched backward, twisted to one side, and her ear-splitting shriek lasted for about a minute and a half. After this her body relaxed and her head returned to an erect position.

"You know," she commented after it was all over, "I felt I was sitting listening to that scream. It was not like it was part of me at all. I can hardly believe it came out of my own mouth."

The next spirit was *allergy* and it came out fairly easily, but to our amazement, there were sixteen other allergic demons in Stella's body. Each of them was an allergy to a specific thing. We all renounced the demons along with Stella. When the *allergy to lilacs* was named, Jenny, our hostess, was also delivered.

"Won't it be wonderful for the first time in my life to be able to walk down a road where there are lilac bushes without ending up in misery!" she exclaimed. It was even better than that. Large bouquets of lilacs were soon all over her house, and Jenny enjoyed them more than anyone else. Not a runny nose, nor an itchy eye, nor any other symptom in relation to lilacs has ever troubled her since.

Another friend present that night was delivered from a

spirit of *allergy to ragweed* at the same time that Stella was. In her case this thing had afflicted her for thirty-five years. Now well over a year later, she reports that she is still completely free of hay fever.

Stella's deliverance was greatly aided by her determination to face the unpleasant truth in her past and in her own behavior and thought patterns. It was a great lesson to all of us. Many come wanting freedom from a particular ailment, habit, or annoyance; but few are willing to change the sick climate in which these things have thrived. When a person is willing to deal with the whole problem as Stella was, he can be as completely delivered.

Stella mentioned that night three books that helped her to gain the insight she needed to face up to some of these things. One of them was *Your Fear of Love* by Marshall Bryant Hodges. After reading it, she learned to accept and love *herself.* This had been a major part of her problem; she could not stand herself.

"Love has to live within you before it can flow out," she told us. "We must accept our own imperfections, or we won't be able to accept those of others. Jesus said 'You shall love your neighbor *as yourself.'* I had to love myself before I was free to love others.

"Two other books that helped me were *The Healing Light* and *The Healing Gifts of the Spirit,* both by Agnes Sanford. In these I learned the importance of the prayer for healing memories. It makes deliverance complete, for then the emotional scars in the subconscious are healed. Thus a combination of exorcism, cleansing, and healing are necessary for full victory. The wounded soul must be made whole."

That night was the last time Stella ever had to ask for a deliverance meeting. Since then, whenever she has been troubled by spirits, she has been able to cast them out of herself. Through these past two years, she has learned a great deal about standing against the wiles of the enemy. Recently we spoke together about this, and I asked her what advice she would give others who might face a long term deliverance like hers.

"Well, first of all," she told me, "I have to check my attitude. Is it in line with the will of God? Do I really want to do what God says I must do? Even if I don't, can I bring my will around to do what God wants? For instance, if there is some place I know I should go but don't feel like it, I say, 'I *will* go.' If the issue is reading Scripture (as it often is), and I don't feel like doing it and am sure I'll get nothing from it anyway, I say, 'I *will* read three chapters of the Word today and everyday.' Then I sit down and do it. Wonder of wonders, I find God blesses me and I get something out of it after all! By this conscious decision, I pit my will against any spirit tempting me to disobey God.

"I also find that after deliverance I have to go out and *act* like it," Stella continued. "I have to believe God. When I was delivered from self-pity, I had quite a battle for a while. It was a great temptation to start feeling sorry for myself every time my husband blasted off about something. However I found I could *will* to stop reacting to him (remembering that he doesn't know Jesus yet and the enemy is trying to use him to defeat me), and *decide* not to feel sorry for myself. And I didn't."

It was thrilling the way the Lord Jesus was teaching this child of God to yield to Him and to resist the devil. The things Stella was saying had the ring of truth to them.

"Do you realize that you have just been sharing with me the practical outworkings of Romans chapter six? Verse sixteen says, 'Do you not know that when you present yourselves to someone as slaves for obedience, you are slaves of the one whom you obey, either of sin resulting in death, or of obedience resulting in righteousness?' What you have been telling me shows this clearly. You find you *must* put your will on the side of God and yield to Him in these matters as they come up, or you could be trapped back into bondage. No wonder some don't stay free. They seem unwilling to face this fact."

"That's a big part of staying free, I admit," Stella agreed, "but there's another way in which people can stay trapped by the enemy too. If demonic leadings are accepted as if they are from God, a person can get into real trouble."

"How well I know," I said ruefully. "My grim experience in 1966 was a direct result of that kind of garbage. I've often wondered since whether God has any warning signals we should see before we go too far."

"He sure does!" Stella said enthusiastically. "One day last year I suspected the devil was giving me ideas and guidance sometimes, but I wasn't absolutely sure. A friend in the group I was with suggested I read 1 John 4:1–3. Here, let me read them to you."

I handed her the Bible on our end table, and she began.

> "Beloved, do not believe every spirit, but test the spirits to see whether they are from God; because many false prophets have gone out into the world. By this you know the Spirit of God: every spirit that confesses that Jesus Christ has come in the flesh is from God; and every spirit that does not confess Jesus is not from God; and this is the spirit of the antichrist, of which you have heard that it is coming, and now it is already in the world.

"I began to take these verses literally. Every time a thought came to me I asked that question under my breath, 'Did Jesus Christ come in the flesh?' The question brought either a yes or a no into my mind immediately. If the answer was yes, then I knew the idea in question was from the Lord; if it was no, then I was equally sure it was from the evil one."

"What if you don't get any answer?" I asked, skeptically.

"Then you do nothing about the idea," she answered. "Probably it came from your own human thoughts, and needs to be weighed against Scripture, circumstance, and the barometer of peace in your heart like all other decisions."

"I'm glad you just said that," I said, closing my eyes and speaking slowly. "There's one big pitfall I could see from this idea. Suppose people began testing the spirits in this way, using it as a kind of gimmick, addressing that question to any thought that popped into their minds. Don't you think some might think they could short-cut God's way?"

"I'm not sure I follow you," Stella said, frankly.

"Well," I went on, opening my eyes and looking out of the window, "I really believe if a person dwells in Scripture and honestly *walks* in all the light God gives him, he would not need to do this very often, to ask the question 'Did Jesus Christ come in the flesh?' Ninety-five percent of the big and little decisions of life are covered by Scripture. Once you know the principle on which God expects you to make a decision, your obedience to Him or willingness to follow Him should lead you to make the right one. We cannot twist the arm of God to make Him ratify our opinions. If a course of thought or action we 'feel led' to take is wrong, no amount of prayer or testing the spirits would make it right. In a case like that where we were seeking wrong guidance (that is, wanting a thing to turn out a certain way to further our own ends), I believe God would give us over to the enemy for his deception."

"Where in the Bible could you back up an idea like that?" Stella asked, a little surprised.

"In the account of Ahab's seeking guidance about whether to go up to Ramoth-gilead to battle or not (1 Kings 22). Remember how determined Ahab was to go? Then he called his four hundred 'yes-men' prophets, and they all predicted what he wanted: victory. However, along comes *God's* prophet—Micaiah—and Ahab gets the whole, unvarnished truth. If he *does* go up to Ramoth-gilead, he will be killed. Furthermore, the revelation didn't end there. Micaiah's vision also included *God's instruction* to a deceiving spirit to entice Ahab to do this very thing by speaking through all his false prophets. You know the end of the story. Bullheaded Ahab went and lost his life."

"How do you feel that applies to testing the spirits in the manner of 1 John 4:1–3, Pat?" Stella asked, quietly.

"Just in the matter of heart attitude or motive, Stella," I said. "God always looks on the heart. If *that's* right, He can do almost anything with us, no matter how much we blunder. But if that's wrong, nothing can ever make our actions right, try as we might. This method you're trying might help us all in some difficult places where we face a fork in the road, provided neither of a couple of conflicting alternatives were unscriptural. In other words, if you felt led to do *two* things, and were vacillating between them, this might help. But just be careful about going to it like 'ouija board Bible guidance,' that's all. . . ."

"What on earth is *that?*" Stella interrupted, incredulously.

"It's this kooky business of opening a Bible, closing your eyes, and putting your finger on a verse," I snorted. "Some people do the same thing with a 'promise box.' God seldom leads that way. There are no short cuts to learning His Word, hiding it in our hearts—and that means memorizing it—or spending time waiting on Him."

"I think I'm beginning to get the message," Stella said, getting up and preparing to go. "Testing the spirits will only work when our *human* spirit agrees with doing God's will. It makes sense. That's another reason we have to be sure to take the ground back from Satan that we gave him in the first place."

"How do you do *that?*" I asked, amazed.

"Just ask God to reveal the ground you or your ancestors gave to the enemy which gave the demons entrance. Ask God's forgiveness and say, 'Satan, I take the ground back from you; that place in my life belongs to the Lord Jesus, now.' "

"Thanks so much for sharing these things, Stella," I said, following her out onto our deck. "Praise God for all He's taught you. I'm sure the only reason He's allowed you to suffer so much was so that He could use you to help many, many others. Just watch the way He'll bring them to you!"

As she backed her car around in our driveway, Stella waved and gave me a radiant smile. No one would ever dream this was the same woman whose face was twisted in torment a few months earlier. What an evidence of the power of Jesus, the great Deliverer!

12
Deliverance of a Child Demoniac

It was just about dusk one balmy June evening on a tidal river of Maryland's eastern shore. The Bartons stood with us on the dock in front of their restored colonial home which must have been at least 150 years old. The stone house sat on a bluff overlooking a small cove where several boats had already anchored for the night. A fiery carpet of twilight glory reached across the gray river to the wharf, the dying sun's bequest to her admirers on the shore. Occasionally a jumping fish broke the enchanted silence, but only for a few seconds. It would disappear quickly underwater, as if embarrassed by its own intrusion into the tableau.

"What a still evening," Dick commented. "It's hard to believe the weather report. Storm warnings are up on both sides of the Chesapeake too."

"Oh, don't let that fool you," Jack said, laughing nonchalantly. "Some of our worst storms come up down here within a half hour's time. It's actually hard to get all the awnings furled in time, and if you don't, you can lose them or wreck them in the high winds."

"Yes, it's a deceptive calm tonight," Louise Barton added. "I'm sure of that. Why don't we go up to the house now? Cindy's waiting for us on the porch."

As we started walking up the gentle slope from the river's edge to the house, we saw a pale, redheaded little girl sitting in a rocker alone on a porch which stretched the full width of the house. There she was—moody, frightened, and withdrawn. Her long hair hung loosely, carelessly about her shoulders; the sallowness of her complexion made her look like a very sick child. She had big, black eyes staring in an anxious way from beneath a shiny, high forehead.

A deceptive calm, I thought.

By the time the Bartons, our two teenage boys, Dick and I were all on the porch, the little girl had begun to rock back and forth feverishly. She made a point of looking at two of the boats down at the end of the cove.

"Cindy," her father said, "here are Mr. and Mrs. Brooks and their sons, Charles and John. Won't you say hello?"

"Hullo," she said sullenly, her face still turned away from us.

"We're glad to meet you, Cindy," I said as cheerfully as I could. "We have come to help you. We are going to ask the Lord Jesus Christ to deliver you from those things which have made life so hard. Do you want us to go inside, or would you rather stay out here on the porch?"

"Let's go inside," Cindy said.

Jack opened the old screen door; it squeaked on its hinges as we all filed past him into the large living room. We sat in the corner of the room nearest the door. Our sons brought in extra chairs from the kitchen so we could all be fairly close together. Cindy sat in a large, plum colored velour chair, sinking back in it and looking from one to the other of us with a frightened-little-rabbit expression on her face. Louise sat very close to her, holding her daughter's spindly little hand in hers.

As soon as we were all seated, Dick began to pray. He claimed the protection of the blood of Jesus Christ on both families and their loved ones, and asked God for wisdom to proceed so that Cindy would be set free from the forces troubling her life. (There was no need for a teaching session with these folks, for they had heard the Basham two-hour tape earlier in the week.) After leading the family in renunciations of the occult, breaking the demonic heredity, and praying prayers of forgiveness, we took authority over the spirits.

"In the name of Jesus Christ, we command all you evil spirits which may be lurking in the life of this young child to come to the surface and identify yourselves, ruler demon first."

Cindy's eyes became dull as soon as this command was given. She looked down and began to fidget nervously with her hands. In a few seconds she looked up again, but this time with an entirely different expression. Her face was contorted, and a look of inexpressible hostility bathed her face. Those in our family realized we were no longer dealing with the child, but with a demon within her.

"Demon, give us your name," I said. "We command you to do so in Jesus' name."

The child's body became rigid, and steely eyes stared at me with deep loathing, but no voice broke the tense silence.

Suddenly the word *hate* flashed into my mind.

"It's a spirit of *hate*, Cindy. Can you hear me?" I asked.

There was no answer from the slender form in the big plum chair. The body began to move in an uneasy way, swaying from side to side; while the hypnotic, vicious eyes riveted their gaze toward mine.

"Cindy, Cindy, can you hear me?" I asked again, this time a little louder.

The child's head jerked back suddenly, and a dazed look came into her eyes. In a weak, little voice she said, "Yes, I hear you."

"Cindy," I went on, "we want you to say something for us. Say, 'I renounce the spirit of *hate* in the name of Jesus.'"

"I—I—I—huh?" she stopped, looking at me thoroughly confused.

"All right, Cindy," I said softly, "you just say it slowly after me. 'I renounce.' "

"I—I—re—re—re . . ." Cindy kept repeating with obvious effort.

"nounce," I added.

"nou—nou—nou—nounce," the child finally stammered out triumphantly.

"the spirit," I went on.

"the s—s—s . . ." Cindy continued. Suddenly she stopped speaking, and hideous laughter came out of her mouth.

"Cindy," I said firmly, "try to listen to me and not to them. Say, 'the spirit.' "

"The sp—sp—spirit," she finally said.

"of *hate*," I persisted.

"of *ha—ha—ha—hate.*" Cindy spat out the word under extreme duress, almost like a deaf person learning to speak.

"In Jesus' name," I finished. By now her parents and our two boys were praying constantly, while Dick and I spoke to the little girl.

"In—in—in Je—Je—Je—Jeeeeeeeeee . . ." The child began to shudder and shake. She could not say the name of Jesus.

"Jesus , Cindy," I said, walking over to her and taking both her hands in mine. "Jesus—Jesus' name."

"Je—Je—Je—Jesus, Jesus' name," she said finally, slumping over in an exhausted heap. Louise was now sitting on the floor just in front of her daughter and holding her in her arms to keep her from sliding off the chair.

"Come out of there, spirit of *hate*," I said, "in the name of the Lord Jesus Christ. '*God* is love; God is love; God is love.' "

I repeated this scripture deliberately, for we had found in other deliverance sessions that it was a powerful weapon against the spirit of *hate*. Often appropriate verses of Scripture will speed the process of deliverance from demon power.

Slumped over on her mother's arms, the child waited passively for a few minutes while we gave the command again a few times. Finally the spirit turned loose with a violent, retching cough.

Cindy sat up in the chair suddenly, with great surprise. For a minute or two the innocent face of the child was before us, but it did not last long. Within a short time her face began to twist and contort again, and soon another evil presence looked out through those black eyes.

"Demon now manifesting," I said, "give us your name."

"*Murder,*" a sly voice said, altogether different from the voice of the little girl. "*Murder,* that's my name."

"Cindy, can you hear us?" I asked the little girl much louder than before. This time there was no answer from the child at all; so we decided to proceed with the ministry without her renunciation of the spirits. By now Cindy's human personality was completely submerged. We decided to renounce the spirits on her behalf, and all of us began commanding the spirit of *murder* to come out.

Outside the rumblings of thunder told us the storm warnings had indeed been authentic. Occasional flashes of lightning came very close to the house, and the boat lights bobbed crazily on the river. Soon the wind came swooping across the water and slung sheets of rain at the windows horizontally like paper spewed from a mimeograph machine.

Inside we had our own kind of storm signals, but unlike the thunder shower, the intensity of the spiritual battle did not stay at any peak. Rather, with the expulsion of each demon spirit from the child's body, the battle completely ebbed, to be replaced by a flow of new manifestations within a minute or two.

When we gave the command the next time, there was no answer, either from the girl or from the demon. Instead, a strange, faraway look came into Cindy's eyes, and she got up, walking behind her father and staring off toward a corner of the room. Suddenly a voice began to talk out of the child, a very agitated woman's voice.

"December 14, 1934," the voice said.

"Where?" several of us asked in unison.

"Nova Scotia," came the self-assured reply. "It's too bad. Bill fell overboard, and now nobody will be able to rescue him. He's gone all right. I can't even see him."

The child's eyes began to look down at a point about ten feet away, as if over the side of a boat.

"Yes, he just fell overboard. It's a windy day and it could happen to anybody on a sixteen-foot sailboat. Of course it could."

As the strange voice went on, the child's hands shot up in front of her, and her eyes began to look back and forth from one to the other of us, first in wonder, and then in horror.

"No, no, that's not the truth," the voice continued. "I pushed him. I pushed him overboard. I killed him. I killed him!"

During the verbal confession, her hands were making violent pushing motions outward in the direction that her eyes had been looking—overboard.

We all sat in stunned amazement at the game of charades being enacted before us. Finally Dick said, "Demon now manifesting, in the name of Jesus we command you to give us your name."

"Yes, I pushed him, and I'm glad I did it," the voice went on, appearing to ignore the command. "He deserved it, fooling around the way he has for the past two years with Mary. And me the last person in town to know! Woe to you, Bill. It's too late for you now."

The hands began the repetitous pushing motions again.

"Dick," I asked, "do you think there could be a *pushing* spirit? She keeps repeating that word over and over again. Perhaps it's the cunning of the demon to obey our command but veil its identity in the hope that it will not be cast out."

At my comments a telltale look of fright crossed the girl's face, and again the eyes that looked in my direction expressed a strange, unearthly hostility.

"Sure seems that way," Dick said. "Let's try it."

"*Pushing* demon, come out in Jesus' name," we said. By now Jack and Louise were entering into the commands and rejoicing in their own authority as believers.

In a minute or two, after several violent, negative shakings of the head, the spirit did come out. The child continued to stand in the middle of the room, her hands up to her head.

"Oh, my head, my head," the woman's voice said again. "It's terrible—the pain, the pain; the awful swirling of the water; the black cold, the awful cold."

The voice changed. It became impossible to hear the rest of the mumbled remarks, so frail and faint were the words.

"Demon, what is your name?" I demanded. "We command you to give it, in the name of Jesus."

The very weak voice moaned, "It's a terrible thing to drown, an awful way to go."

We commanded the spirit of *drowning* to go and it left with a long, low moan. The eyes of the child grew bright again, and she began to look around her (in front, to the left, to the right—but always downward) with a strange, almost hypnotic fascination in her eyes.

"There's so much of it here all around me," the woman's voice said again. "All around me, so much water. That's why I love it here, because of the water."

"Do you think there could be a spirit of *water?*" Jack asked incredulously, as his daughter's eyes smiled rapturously at the floor.

"It's worth a try," I said. "Demon of *water,* come out of her in the name of the Lord Jesus Christ."

With a series of short, staccato coughs, this demon turned loose after a few minutes of commanding. Then suddenly without any warning, Cindy's body slipped to the floor. She had fainted.

Dick got up quickly, picked her up and gently carried the pale, unconscious child to the couch. Louise cried out in anguish at this evidence of her child's ordeal; Jack knelt at her side, his arms about her, trying to comfort her.

In a few moments Cindy's eyelids began to flutter; the body began to writhe restlessly, and her right fist clenched as if over a knife. Resolutely the hand was brought up just over the child's heart, and began making terrible stabbing motions in a steady, forceful rhythm. With each plunge of the imaginary knife, her face contorted unbelievably.

"It hurts. It hurts so much," a tortured, rasping voice said as her head was wrenched violently and grotesquely upward toward the arm of the couch. With each stab of the clenched fist, color drained from her complexion—not face only, but arms, neck, and legs. Soon a corpse-like pallor spread through Cindy's whole body as we stood spellbound by the sight.

By now Louise was sobbing hysterically into her husband's shoulder as he held her in his arms. Suddenly Dick, the boys, and I came to our senses. "Demon of *suicide*, come out of Cindy right now in the name of the Lord Jesus Christ."

With a deep, hoarse cough, the demon left at once, and the "corpse" sat bolt upright on the couch, her color returning to normal. The death scene, a terrible ordeal to watch, had now shifted to act two.

"That was Mary, the other woman," a cunning female voice said. "She deserved it; she was the real trouble maker. I'm glad it hurt so much. That fiend had no right to him; he was mine, he had no right to look at another woman."

We tossed the spirit of *jealousy* out matter-of-factly, and he left with an earsplitting, guilty shriek. Now the voice coming from the child's mouth changed, and her eyes began to move up and down in a kind of bewitched horror, staring at something she appeared to see on the walls.

"What do you see?" I asked. "Demon now manifesting, give us your name."

"Well, it's no good to see them here because I can't see any more on that program. Cindy won't let me now, and her parents won't, either—you'll find out!"

"What program?" Dick and Jack demanded, in unison. "Give us your name, demon."

Putting both arms stiffly out to one side, the child's eyes were riveted on to her own fingertips as they were drawn back slowly in front of her.

"*Dark Shadows,*" she said, dramatically.

"That's its name," I said. "Come out of her in the name of Jesus, spirit of *dark shadows.*" (This was the name of a TV drama series.)

The child began to scream with a new kind of pain. She picked up her right foot which had curled downward in a grotesque way and laid it gingerly on her left knee, moaning all the while.

"Demon, name yourself," Dick ordered.

"*Feet,*" came a defiant voice.

"That couldn't be it," I said skeptically. "It must be *defeat* or something like that."

"I said *feet!*" the voice yelled. Eyes glared at me, "You deaf or something? That's my name, *feet: f,e,e,t—feet!*"

"How could that be?" one of our boys asked. "How could you have a spirit of *feet?*"

"Oh!" Louise, now fully recovered from her shock during the "suicide," said suddenly. "This could explain a lot of things. Cindy was born with deformed feet, and she had three operations before she was a year old. Remember, Jack, the pain she had—especially with the foot she is holding now?"

"That's right," Jack said in low-voiced wonder. "Do you think that could have been in the child when she was born?"

"Sure I was," the harsh voice bragged. "Most of us were here when she was born."

"We've heard enough from you," I said. "Spirit of *feet,* come out of Cindy right now in the name of Jesus Christ."

The answer was a low moan from Cindy as she clutched the foot even more tightly, her body shuddering down further and further until her head lay on top of the painful foot on her knee. Then the demon left with one last yell of complaint, and the child sat up, relaxed again.

The next spirit gave us a few syllables in French and began to speak of Paris and French Canada in knowing terms, expressing a desire to go back. Here again Louise's revelation was almost hard to believe.

"Cindy was able to speak French before she ever spoke English," she reminisced wistfully. "Before she was a year old, she spoke sentences of French, despite the fact that nobody in our family knew French. We have some French Canadian ancestors, but she never knew them."

"Didn't you think that was a little *strange?*" I asked in amazement. "I mean, a toddler able to speak a foreign language she never learned?"

"No, I really didn't," Louise said, blushing as she looked down. Her hands were nervously fingering a handkerchief which Jack had given her a few minutes ago while she was crying. "We were with a healing group that was in our church at the time. They believed in reincarnation and were involved with eastern religions as well as Christianity. They said she had just come back from another life in which she was French, and we believed that."

"A French Bridey Murphy, you mean?" Dick asked smiling.

"Well, some of what we've seen tonight would probably convince a person who believed in reincarnation that he was right," Jack said.

"That's true," I said. "Those who are blinded by Satan will interpet things in the light of their deception. But for the Christian, Jack, there is only one explanation. It is the one the demons have given, themselves, when under the command of those with absolute authority over them in Christ. Demons who have indwelt other people in other places and times get into a contemporary body and express themselves. In fact, this is why they desperately seek human bodies. Since they are disincarnate spirits, they must have human bodies in order to express their wretched personalities. Tonight I believe we have seen evidence of demons, converged in this child's body, from three separate people in Nova Scotia who were involved in a marital triangle in 1934."

"How did they have the *right* to do it?" Louise asked passionately.

"Your involvement with reincarnation didn't exactly help," I said as gently as I could.

"Oh, I'm sorry for that now. God knows I'm sorry!" Louise said, burying her face in her hands and starting to cry again softly.

"Will we ever get her *completely* back?" Jack asked, taking out his handkerchief and blowing his nose several times as he held his wife's hand.

"Yes, we will get her back," I said quietly. "In a few minutes the storm will be over outside, and we'll be able to see the boats again. And soon the spiritual storm will be over inside, and we'll be able to talk to Cindy again. Right now we have more work to do."

By midnight it was peaceful both outside and inside the Barton home. Thirty-five spirits had been cast out and Cindy was cuddled on her father's lap.

Finally her own voice said, "I'm sleepy, Daddy. Can I go to bed?" Though none of us was convinced the job was completely done, we were all very tired and decided to call it a night, praise the Lord, and get together in the morning. Each of us would continue to fast until lunch time.

As soon as we took authority over the spirits Saturday morning, Cindy's human personality was submerged again and the remaining demons resumed their show for our benefit. The one that took the longest time and had puzzled us the night before was a spirit that kept drawing smiles on all of our faces. With a silly grin Cindy would point to each of us in succession moving her hand in a *U* in front of our mouths. We guessed a *smiling* spirit, but that was not it. Finally Jack and I both got the word *madness* at the same time, and we commanded it out in Jesus' name.

As soon as the demon was accurately named, the idiotic grin was replaced with a haunted, found-out look of great disappointment, and it came out with a scream worthy of the attic scene in *Jane Eyre*.

After the psychotic demon left, Cindy's own personality returned to the surface. From then on she was able to renounce the spirits and cooperate in her own deliverance, which seemed to speed up the whole process. But before long the ministry came to a standstill. We knew we were not yet finished, for Cindy had a sickish feeling and was trembling all over.

The Lord and Deliverer knew what was wrong, so we all went to prayer and asked Him to show us. Someone got the word *unforgiveness* as our answer, and Cindy then asked God to show her whom she needed to forgive. The names of five playmates came to her mind at once; she told the Lord she was sorry and forgave them one by one in Jesus' name.

After that the spirits left in rapid succession, barely giving her time to renounce them. By noon she was free and radiantly happy for the first time in her ten years of life.

Today the Barton home is being used of God for the deliverance of others the Lord sends their way. Each member of the family has been baptized in the Holy Spirit, and often it is Cindy who receives the word that unlocks a difficult case.

God is still illustrating His Word with living examples. "And a little child shall lead them . . ." as stated in Isaiah 11:6 (*KJV*) has again proved true.

13

The Friday Night Prayer Meetings

By July of 1970 we realized there was need to provide a regular time for deliverance meetings. People were calling us at all hours of the day and night for help. Often we would see them soon after they called. Before long our family life became hectic, and it was hard for me to get even the food shopping and minimum housework done.

Since school was out now, it was imperative for me to have more time for my children. Dick and I prayed about the problem, and decided to set Friday night as a regular time when deliverance needs could be met. We began the prayer meetings in the middle of that summer and have seen the Lord bless them ever since.

At first Dick was reluctant to take a leadership role in the deliverance ministry, but that fall he began to assume authority more and more. He experienced the fullness of the Holy Spirit himself when Don Basham again came into our area, and from that time on led groups in the renunciations against the occult and in commands for the spirits to manifest themselves and leave.

We have followed a certain pattern with people who cal
us inquiring about deliverance. First we ask them to hear the
two-hour Don Basham tape on the subject; then if they are
still interested, we suggest that they join us during the Friday
night prayer meeting.

After a time of praise, singing, and prayer, Dick or one of
the other men in our New Testament Fellowship leads the
group in the following prayers:

Thank you, Lord, for dying for my sins, for your glorious
resurrection, and for making me a new creature in Christ
by faith in your precious blood.

Dear Lord, I have a confession to make:

I have sought supernatural experience apart from you.

I have disobeyed your Word.

I want you to help me renounce all these things and cleanse
me in body, soul, and spirit in Jesus' name.

I renounce witchcraft and magic, both black and white.

I renounce ouija boards and all other occult games.

I renounce all seances, clairvoyance, and mediums.

I renounce ESP (extrasensory perception), second sight, and
mind reading.

I renounce all fortune telling: palm reading, tea leaf reading,
crystal balls, Tarot or other card laying.

I renounce all astrology and interest in horoscopes.

I renounce the heresy of reincarnation and all contacts with
demonic healing groups having an interest in it.

I renounce all hypnosis under any excuse or authority.

I renounce all curiosity about either future or past, and which
is outside Thy will.

I renounce water witching or dowsing, levitation, body lifting,
table tipping, psychometry, and automatic writing.

I renounce all literature I have ever read in any of these
fields.

I now break, in the name of the Lord Jesus Christ, all psychic
heredity, and any demonic hold upon my family line as a
result of disobedience in any of these areas by any of my
ancestors.

In the Name of Jesus Christ I renounce everything psychic and
occult.

I renounce every cult that denies the blood of Christ.

I renounce every philosophy that denies the divinity of Christ.

I call upon the Lord to set me free.

Lord, I have another confession to make:

I have held resentment against people.

I call upon you, Lord, to help me forgive them.

I do now forgive

(Here we all put in the names of those the Lord brings to mind and forgive them on the spot.)

I do now forgive myself.

I renounce every evil spirit that binds or torments me, and I call upon the Lord to set me free.

After these introductory prayers are said after the leader by the whole group, someone present prays the prayer of protection under the blood of Jesus Christ for every member of every family represented. We trust God, through this prayer, to keep any angered spirits from entering others after they leave those who are being delivered.

Then Dick, or whoever is in charge, takes authority over the spirits in a manner something like this: "In the name of Jesus Christ I take authority over you, Satan, and over all you demons tormenting anyone present. I command you to come to the surface and name yourselves and then come out, ruler demon first."

(We are indebted to Kenneth Hagin's book *Ministering to the Oppressed* for our understanding of the importance of locating and evicting the ruler spirit. The Lord showed Hagin that one demon exercises the major control over a human personality in any given case and opens the door for all others which gain entrance into the life. Also, the *New American Standard Bible* makes it clear in Ephesians 6:12 that the first class of spirits we wrestle with are "rulers." Experience has confirmed these findings. We are learning that when a person identifies the ruler spirit, he must not only cast it out; he must also yield that area of his life to the Lord and learn Scripture verses so that he may stand firm against its reentrance into his life. See the back of this book for an

appendix of helpful verses to memorize and use agains
ruler demons.)

One night that first year of the Friday prayer meetings
two very disturbed women came for help. Although they di
not know each other, it was evident that God had arrange
for them to come at the same time; He is a great economist
They had many of the same problems and were frequentl
delivered of spirits with the same name at the same time
During the meeting quite a number of spirits were cast out

Before they went home, we instructed both of them, as w
try always to do, to get into the regular, systematic study o
the Word of God right away. We shared our conviction with
them that the one who has had demons cast out must walk
very close to the Lord afterward, fully submitting to Him and
shunning sin with its old attitude patterns, providing no
further basis for trouble.

I gave them my personal method for reading through the
Scriptures once a year, which requires an average of three
chapters daily and five on Sunday. In 1958 I heard Roy
Gustafson recommend this way of staying in Scripture and
can endorse his enthusiasm thoroughly since I have been
using it ever since.

Very simply, this system divides the Bible into six major
portions from which the daily readings are taken for the six
weekdays. On Monday at least three chapters are read from
the Pentateuch (Genesis to Deuteronomy); on Tuesday,
three chapters from the historical books (Joshua to Esther);
on Wednesday, a similar amount from the poetical books
(Job to Song of Solomon); on Thursday from the prophets
(Isaiah to Malachi); on Friday from the gospels (Matthew to
John); and on Saturday from the rest of the New Testament.
Sunday I use either to catch up or read ahead.

Every day when I finish my reading for that day, I put the
date in pencil at the end of the chapter where I stopped.
Then I know where to start reading a week later, at which
time I erase the old date, begin reading from there, and date
the new place where I stop. Whenever I come across a date
two or three weeks old, I realize I have been backsliding and
have some catching up to do.

The plan is fascinating, for one is familiar with all major portions of the Scripture at the same time. There is no need for a printed schedule nor is there any limit as to how many or how few chapters are read. This system adjusts perfectly to our fluctuating daily schedules.

That night only one of the women heeded our warning. Sarah (we shall call her) took us at our word, got right into a Bible study group, and began her own private study as just outlined. She also followed our instruction to continue to take authority over spirits at home as they troubled her, and cast them out of herself.

In the weeks that followed, Sarah became progressively more free. Soon she knew a joy which she had never experienced before although she had been a believer since childhood. Before long she had a release in the prayer language she had been given that first Friday night at our home when we all laids hands on her. Since that time Sarah has seen two members of her family come to Christ and is trusting God for the salvation of her husband and other children.

The other woman, however, did nothing to stand against the enemy. She did not study the Bible daily or continue in Christian fellowship with any small group for study and prayer. Soon all her old torment was back, and she began to criticize and find fault with those who had tried to help her. The difference between these women, both of whom had many of the same demons cast out on the same night, vividly points out how important it is to make Jesus absolute lord of life and to stand against Satan.

On another Friday night a pastor's wife from another area came to us. She was suffering from various bodily ailments as well as deep feelings of insecurity and was genuinely worried about her difficulty in concentrating.

Carrie had much trouble with the renunciations, stopping and stammering constantly throughout. We had to go very slowly for her, pleading the blood (repeating the phrase *the blood of Jesus* several times) and praying for her so that she could get the words out.

The ruler demon was apparently *self-pity*. Once it was named, she shared an incident from her childhood which had proved traumatic. This is a frequent occurrence during times of deliverance. Often the demons do not leave until the incident which occasioned their entrance has been revealed. Perhaps a healing takes place at this point. At any rate, such happenings help to show why such scientific disciplines as psychiatry and psychology do surely have their place.

After telling us her story, Carrie coughed slightly and felt somewhat relieved for about one minute. We assumed that the demon of *self-pity* left at that point, but another one began to manifest almost immediately. Carrie began to breathe heavily, her eyes closed and her head swaying back and forth. When we asked the demon to give its name, Carrie gave the word *loneliness*.

As soon as the word passed her lips, however, she fainted and slipped to the floor like a rag doll. We picked her up, and put her on the bed in the next room, and continued to cast out the demons for an hour and a half. All of the demons spoke out of her; many of them were argumentative, vicious, and snarling. Any doubters present must have been convinced of the reality of demons that night, for Carrie's own personality is demure and self-controlled.

When the demon *schizophrenia* named itself, it shook her head and vowed it would never come out. Despite the fact that we repeated the commands, pled the blood, and sang a number of usually effective songs. Carrie's body continued to thrash back and forth on the bed in obvious torment.

Finally it occurred to us that this spirit had a hold on her life which would have to be released before it would go. We addressed the spirit directly, "You schizophrenic demon, on what basis do you stay in this girl's life? Tell us your ground for being there; we command you in Jesus' name."

A peculiar low moan was emitted from Carrie's lips and her eyes looked up vaguely toward a corner of the room as she swayed back and forth against the pillow propped up behind her.

"It's—it's the fact that she sleeps too much," a petulant, childish voice answered.

"You're lying, demon," I said sharply. "Tell me the truth in Jesus' name."

Another moan came from the swaying body propped up against the pillows.

"It's—it's . . ." the same voice said, as the eyes closed and the face contorted in agony, *"unclean imaginations."*

At this point the body suddenly lurched toward the side of the bed, and the girl was thrown on her stomach as the demons attempted to push her off onto her head. Several of us grabbed her just in time, and she began to pound her fist against the side of the bed, crying and yelling in a most unladylike manner. We took authority over the spirit of *unclean imaginations;* then a whole series of sex demons were named and came out one by one. Many of these were released with vomiting, and we had to run for the paper towels and the large plastic bowl we keep in the kitchen for this purpose. After the demons were gone, however, Carrie's personality returned to the surface with a new sweetness and liberty not evident when she had come to the house earlier that night.

"You know," she said as she put on her coat, "if I hadn't been conscious through at least part of this, I would never have believed what happened to me here tonight! To think that my husband *laughed* when I told him I just spent my day sitting and staring at the walls. It was the truth! Why, if I hadn't gotten rid of those demons, I'd have landed in a mental institution before long. Praise Jesus for this marvelous deliverance!"

Over the past two years our family room has been the scene of many victories like those of Sarah and Carrie. It has also been the scene of ministry which resulted in no permanent improvement, such as in the case of the other girl who was here with Sarah. Why? Does God play favorites?

Certainly not! God runs His universe in order and precision. As someone has said, no one breaks God's laws, but many are broken by them. The principle here is found in

3 John:2, "Beloved, I pray that in all respects you may prosper and be in good health, *just as your soul prospers.*" No permanent healing or deliverance is possible where the rudder of the human will continually steers the human personality into the wind on a course in direct opposition to the will of God.

A poignant example of this was Ann, a cancer patient who first was brought to us at a Friday night prayer meeting. Ann was born again about a year before we met her and had great faith and courage throughout her illness. She had a desire for healing, and even flew to a distant city once to hear Kathryn Kuhlman. Many local prayer groups were asking God for a miracle on her behalf; yet healing strangely eluded her.

Although Ann made a clean break with her occult past which had been extensive, she never came to the place where her soul was at peace; she had never won a final battle over resentment and unforgiveness. I visited her in the hospital when she was very ill, and was startled to hear her use her small reserve of strength recounting her husband's faults.

"This is doing you no good, Ann," I said softly, but as firmly as I could. "When he comes in here tonight, you had better forgive him for everything."

"Why?" she asked in a dazed way. "Why should I forgive him after all he's done to me?"

"Because you want God to forgive you," I answered her. "God cannot forgive us if we hold a grudge toward any other human being. He has limited Himself in this way. It is a law He has written into this universe, just as irrevocable as, say, the law of centrifugal force. When you go to meet Him, you don't want a barrier of unforgiveness between yourself and Him."

"All right, I will," she said, in a resigned sort of way.

Apparently God had been waiting for this breakthrough, for He took her out of this world to His home the very next day.

Some of us felt the Lord answered the desire of her heart by allowing her to die. Although Ann wanted to share the companionship of her children, she was not really looking forward to living with her husband. A return to health would have involved facing this issue in a final way—a change of attitude which she was either unwilling or unable to make at that point.

Two other cancer cases for whom we have prayed in our New Testament Fellowship were dramatically healed of every trace of the dread disease—to the consternation and amazement of the doctors involved—and neither one ever appeared at our prayer meeting. All the prayer was done from a distance, and in each case we commanded the demon of *cancer* to depart right here, in absentia.

Why such different answers to prayer? No one can say for sure, since God is sovereign and can do exactly as He wills in each individual case. However, Ann's case did leave us some clues about the importance of attitudes and relationships toward the prospering of the soul.

In the following chapter, failures in deliverance will be examined—the most difficult part of such a ministry. We have seen a number of people who have had evil spirits cast out and have become worse afterward. Anyone who is in this ministry must honestly admit to this fact. Jesus Himself warned of this very possibility in Matthew 12:43–45.

> Now when the unclean spirit goes out of a man, it passes through waterless places, seeking rest, and does not find it. Then it says, "I will return to my house from which I came"; and when it comes, it finds it unoccupied, swept, and put in order. Then it goes, and takes along with it seven other spirits more wicked than itself, and they go in and live there; and the last state of that man becomes worse than the first. That is the way it will also be with this evil generation.

The word *unoccupied* provides the key for unlocking this passage. Most emphatically, the Lord Jesus did not give this warning to keep people from obeying His clear command to cast out demons in His name (Matthew 10:1, Mark 3:14, 15; Mark 16:17; Luke 10:17–20). God is never inconsistent. What He was saying is that a life not filled with the Spirit of God and the Word of God is inviting reentry of evil spirits even after exorcism.

No initial experience is enough to guarantee such protection. No matter how dramatic the initial conversion, the deliverance from demons, or the baptism in the Holy Spirit, only the walk in the Spirit *day by day* will keep a person free. Obedience to the Word of God and the flow of the light-producing oil of God's Spirit in our lives are our only sure guarantees of spiritual freedom.

God's power is not magic. In fact, it is the very antithesis of the evil satanic art of that name. God never by-passes the human will, but always works in cooperation with it. Satan's entire program depends on the opposite premise: he subjugates the human will, invading it not for the purpose of cooperation, but for compulsion.

The Almighty is not interested in puppets, but in sons. The Lord will not manipulate strings in a man's life to force him to come to Him, but He *will* offer to cut the fetters which have bound that man to invisible forces of evil. Either man chooses light, which he finds in Christ, or darkness, which he keeps through sheer passivity. Satan's way involves doing what comes naturally; it is just that simple.

The problems come for the cake eaters who want to hang on not only to their loot, but also to their sweet tooth! Like Scarlet O'Hara they are not really sorry for their wrongdoing, only for getting caught.

Such sailors on life's seas often founder on the rocks of delusion. They imagine God will save them *in* their sin, rather than *from* their sin. Yet the channel is clearly marked by the harbor lights of the Word of God. It is impossible to change God; He can never be made to wink at man's rebellion and disobedience. Indeed His whole redemptive purpose is concerned with delivering man from this ancient snakebite of sin, replacing the fatal darkness with the life-giving light of His Son.

The account in the next chapter is not pleasant reading but is necessary if we are to present a true spectrum of contemporary experience with those seeking deliverance. It is a common error to use such a testimony to denounce the entire miraculous moving of God in these last days. However, to condemn marriage because a few fail is the act of a fool. It is equally absurd to censure this ministry of casting out demons because a few souls prefer to be magnetized by darkness rather than to exert the necessary effort to pull away from the magnetic field. Ultimately, both marriages and deliverances probably fail for the same reason: God's conditions for their success have never been met.

14

"The Last State, Worse Than the First"

One late spring night in 1971 our phone rang. The female voice at the other end of the wire sounded frightened, almost desperate. Heidi was in great need and admitted that she was calling me only as a last resort.

For ten days this young married woman had been suffering from a terrible headache which baffled her doctor. Aspirin would not touch it; even combination pills with codeine had only a slight effect.

Jim, her husband, had phoned a man known for his prayer for the sick earlier in the evening. He had come by with a friend, and together they had laid hands on Heidi, asking the Lord to heal her. As soon as these hands touched her head, Heidi said the pain became unbearable.

"Oh, Pat," she moaned, "Can you help me? It must be demonic, or it wouldn't get worse with the prayer for healing and the laying on of hands. What do you think?"

"I agree. Probably it is demonic," I said. "How come you took so long to come to this conclusion? Didn't you attend a deliverance meeting last fall with Jim?"

"Yes," she answered reluctantly. "But I had trouble believing in all that stuff. I coughed a few times and you thought some demons came out, but it all seemed pretty silly to me at the time. To tell you the truth, I thought you were a kook."

"What brought about your change of heart?" I asked, probing her motives to see if there were any clue as to whether she yet had a will to be free.

"The pain in my head, that's what!" She snapped back at me. As I prayed silently, asking the Lord for guidance, she wailed in agony, "Why can't you cast the demons out over the phone?"

"Well—I have done that," I admitted, "but I'm not sure it's always the greatest idea."

"Why not?" she asked. "If they respond to the word of command, what difference does it make? If you could just feel my head right now, you wouldn't put me off."

"Okay," I agreed, against my better judgment. "Since you renounced the occult and broke the demonic heredity last spring, why don't you just ask the Lord whom you need to forgive, and then forgive them as I pray the prayers of protection on both our families."

When Heidi had forgiven several people, I took authority over the spirits. For several seconds there was silence at the other end of the wire. Then she spoke in a very uncertain voice.

"I don't know. About all I can think of right now are the people I hate. One after another, they keep popping into my mind."

Why I did not stop right there and tell her she was no candidate for deliverance until that hate was in the *past* tense, I'll never know. At any rate, I was fairly sure we had located the ruler demon and decided to try to cast it out on the spot.

"*Hate* is a ruler demon, Heidi," I instructed her. "Just say, 'I renounce the spirit of *hate* in the name of Jesus Christ,' then I'll cast it out."

There was no answer at the other end of the wire, but after about two minutes of silence, I heard a sound of scuffling.

"Heidi?" I asked. "Are you still there?"

"Hi, Pat," a deep male voice said. "This is Jim. Heidi's on the floor unconscious, wriggling around almost like she's in a fit. What do we do now?"

"Oh, oh," I said ruefully. "Let me go downstairs and get Dick. He's working in the garage so it will take him a few minutes to get the grease off his hands. Unless you hear otherwise, expect us there in about forty minutes."

All the way into Schenectady, it seemed that still, small voice of God was reminding me He had warned me about doing this on the phone. What if the man who called me from Dayton, Ohio, the week before had fallen down on the floor? Who would have helped him?

Okay, Lord, I prayed. *I get the message. Never again.*

When we got to the young couple's house, Heidi was conscious, but quite vague. As soon as we took authority over the spirits, *confusion* was named and cast out. *Deception* came next; then a nasty bunch of sex demons began to manifest, and we had to cast them out without her cooperation in renouncing them. Each one of these put up quite a fight, and several times it took real effort for the men to hold her down or keep her from hurting herself.

As the demon *masturbation* left her, Heidi's whole lower body shuddered and went through the apparent motions of having an orgasm, despite the fact that her hands were securely pinned down.

When the *lesbian* demon came to the surface, she began to stroke her own breasts and opened her eyes. A strange, unearthly, and highly suggestive stare was directed at me, the only woman present, until the thing came out on command with an earsplitting shriek.

As the *suicide* demon was leaving, it attempted to strangle her with her own hands. Jim and Dick had to exert powerful effort to disentangle her vise-like fingers from her throat, one at a time.

By three A.M. we were all exhausted. We decided everyone needed some rest. Jim put Heidi to bed, and Dick and I went home.

Since Heidi still felt very disturbed and in need of help in the morning, Beverly and Stella drove into Schenectady to get her. The headache was still terrible, and she had great difficulty trying to walk. The women found it a real job to get her up the stairs to our back door.

We took Heidi to our first floor bedroom and put her on the bed with a blanket over her. When I took authority over the spirits, we immediately lost contact with Heidi's human personality.

The Lord so ordered it that one of my teenage sons was home from school that day. Without him we could not have handled the situation, for the tormented girl soon became violent.

It was a long, exasperating ordeal—not only timewise, but in the response pattern to our commands. Very few of the demons named themselves. However, the Lord impressed their names upon our minds through the gift of the discerning of spirits. Each time we would speak out the right name, the young woman's face would register real fear. Then the violent writhing motions would begin again. Most of the demons thrashed Heidi's body about for twenty minutes or longer before coming out.

Singing "There's Power in the Blood" proved to be our most effective weapon during the many hours we worked with Heidi. After we got hoarse I remembered we had a Jerome Hines recording of it. My son John made a tape of it from the record, and from then on we let our talented brother unsettle the demons while the rest of us used our strength to hold the thrashing body down.

Two things stand out in my memory about that day. First, the unbelievable terror on the girl's face before each demon was forced to leave her body and the obvious dread as it evidently entered into another state. No one who observed this phenomenon could doubt the reality of hell.

Second, these demons seemed to have such an awful hold on her. Could it be that the light, skeptical way Heidi had treated her initial deliverance brought them back sevenfold? Was her renunciation of the occult genuine? We decided to try to find out what was wrong.

"Demon now manifesting," I finally said, "on what grounds do you stay in this girl in the face of the authority we have over you in the name of the Lord Jesus Christ? He defeated you completely on the cross of Calvary, and Heidi is a child of God by faith in Him. Why do you linger?"

"We have a right," a surly voice answered. "She gave it to us."

"How?" I persisted.

"By her phony, incomplete surrender, that's how," the defiant voice said. "She encourages her friend Terri to come over. She doesn't want to break it up; she only says she does."

Beverly, Stella, and I looked at each other in amazement. We were well aware of the problem with Terri who had been a persistent nuisance to Heidi and Jim for some time. Terri was deeply involved with the occult, and even hung a horoscope calendar in Heidi's home despite Jim's objections. One thing especially ominous about Terri was an insistence on bringing Heidi gifts, many of which were stolen. It pointed to the now rather obvious fact that Terri's interest in Heidi was a sexual one, although perhaps Heidi was unaware of this. All Heidi had told us was that Terri made her uncomfortable and left her severely depressed every time she came.

After school was out, my other teenage son, Charlie, joined us. Soon after that Chuck Strott also came over looking for his wife. These two big males were able to take over the pinning down operation, for we women and Johnny were very weary by then. Chuck confessed later that that experience convinced him of the reality of the deliverance ministry; before having to exert all his strength and weight to hold tiny Heidi down, he had discounted casting out demons as bunk.

Friday's ministry continued late into the night. Jim came to help after work, and Dick, Chuck, our boys and Jim got a very thorough physical workout between supper time and the wee hours of the morning. Providentially, the most violent demons came out during this period: *hate, rebellion, murder, strangulation, violence, sadism,* and *masochism.*

On Saturday the men were all busy with other commitments, and the demons were no longer violent; so Beverly, Stella, and I found ourselves working with Heidi again. She had taken no food or water in twenty-four hours, and we got her into the bathroom only twice in that period. It became apparent as soon as we again took authority over the remaining spirits, that the demons named were all in the realm of physical ailments. Evidently the attitude and appetite demons had to come out before these were able to. The first spirit to come out Saturday was *infirmity,* often a key to this whole group.

Saturday's ministry was very orderly. In fact at no time in the two and a half days with Heidi were we reduced to guesswork. The Holy Spirit equips us to do the job God wants done. On this last day Heidi would point to the part of her body where the particular afflictive spirit lodged, then she would moan in pain. Immediately after this the name would be given to one or more of us.

Once she touched a certain part of her head and cried in agony. This proved to be a spirit of *brain tumor,* and once it left, the two-week-old headache went with it. Even the demons reported that the awful head pain was now gone.

At four o'clock in the afternoon, when only Stella and I were left with her, a very weak voice finally said, "It's me, Pat, Heidi."

How thrilled and relieved we were. Sure enough, the expression on the face was finally a human expression again, and the voice was Heidi's voice.

"Well, Heidi," Stella said, "it's good to have you back. You've been gone for quite a while."

"Really?" Heidi seemed surprised. "The last thing I remember is Pat taking authority over the spirits a little while ago. Is is still morning?"

"That was yesterday morning. It's now Saturday afternoon a little after four."

"Wow!" she exclaimed. "Say, my headache is all gone. What do you think of that?"

"Great!" Stella answered sitting down on the edge of the

bed and taking Heidi's hand. "Listen, I have to get home to make my husband's supper, but before I go I want to share something I think will help keep all this mess from coming back into your life."

"You mean they could come back?" Heidi asked amazed.

"Sure," Stella said positively, "and they'll certainly try. They've had a terrible hold on you. The only way you can keep them out is to yield to Jesus as Lord—and that means *boss*. Make up your mind to line up your will firmly with God's will as revealed in His Word. Read at least three chapters of Scripture a day and memorize at least one verse. But don't just study; *do what it says.* Break off all wrong relationships. Begin with that Terri character; get Jim to take back all the gifts she gave you, and don't either of you ever let her in the house again. Be *sure* to submit to your husband."

"What about when Jim's wrong?" Heidi interrupted. "What then? Do I still have to submit to him?"

"Yes!" Stella came back without hesitating. "Submit to anything but sin. You know as well as I do, the usual faults men make are not in that category."

"Why is it so important to submit to him?" Heidi asked a little petulantly.

"Because God keeps your head and mind covered by him in some wonderful way I don't pretend to understand. All I know is, the Lord's method works. If I hadn't learned that lesson before my deliverance started, I never could have stood against the multitude that had invaded my life. And incidentally, you have a big advantage since your husband is a believer; mine isn't."

Heidi looked first at Stella, then at me, then out of the window. The sun was shining brightly, and the tops of the locust trees were just coming into bloom. After a long, lingering winter, here was a sure sign of spring about ready to give way to summer.

As I went to phone Jim, who had been home with their children all day, Stella prayed with Heidi, gave her a hug, and left. I brought her a big glass of orange juice and settled back in the chair next to the bed.

"Boy, I sure am weak," Heidi commented as she handed me the empty juice glass. "Even though my headache is gone, my body feels like I've spent hours on a medieval stretching rack being tortured. What did you people do to me?"

"We didn't do it," I answered slowly. "All we did was try to hold you down. The demons had you wrenching, leaping, and twisting so that we were concerned about the possibility of broken bones. Countless times they tried to push your head through that headboard or throw you off onto the floor despite everything we did to hold you."

"Wow!" Heidi commented in wonder. "Guess I'll have the reminder of that for some time in these aches and pains."

"Well," I said, "maybe that's a good thing, because you don't want to forget how serious this has been. Remember what happened after you took it all so lightly last fall? It looks like you not only got those demons back, but many more besides—although some of this problem has doubtless been with you since childhood. If you look over this list we've written down of the demons from which you have been delivered, you must surely realize that you are going to have to walk *very* close to the Lord. It's not going to be enough to read the Bible and memorize verses. You must *do* what God says. Determine to stand against that ruler demon *hate* by walking in love and depending on the grace of God to respond with love to every situation. Confess every resentment as sin as soon as it happens in your heart. And forgive, forgive, forgive."

During the next six months several people were praying for Heidi. Jim spent part of every evening in the Scripture with her, following the same study schedule Dick and I use. She was doing fairly well for a while. Then she dropped out of the small, concerned church group where they were being fed the Word of God, confiding to me that she just "didn't like the pastor."

This seemed to be a storm warning to me, and I told her

so. It was the very attitude which would give the spirit of *hate* ground. However, she would not listen to me or anyone else, and soon the list of unapproved personalities grew. Poor Jim came in for her most devastating rancor, however. In her opinion he was not worthy to be the head of the house; so she stopped submitting to him. When her attitude opposed the clear teaching of the Word of God in this way, she came out from under the protective covering God has provided for wives to keep them safe from demonic control. (This subject will be covered fully later, in the chapter on getting the home in order.)

Soon afterward, Heidi left her husband and began sending him hate mail. This was heartbreaking for Jim, who finally stopped opening the letters.

If this were a book of fairy tales, this chapter would end, "they both lived happily ever after." However, only in the never-never land does wishing make it so. The stories in this book are not picturesque folk tales embellished by downright fantasy. They are real-life accounts—glimpses of starkly naked truth and stern reality.

No human being is a match for the cunning of the demons. We are to "be strong *in the Lord*, and in the strength of His might" (Ephesians 6:10). Unless we submit to Jesus as *Lord* and acknowledge with the Jesus people that there is "one way" (*His* way irrevocably integrated with His Person) there is no hope.

The saddest development we have had to face in recent months is the shifting position and conviction of two men of God formerly much used in the ministry of casting out demons. Yesterday a woman came to me in heartbroken wonder asking why people going to these men now can no longer get the same help.

Who can doubt that this is the work of deceiving spirits? Having crept back into a life, they begin a subtle whisper campaign against spiritual warfare.

History is rich with eloquent evidence against their fallacy. Not until the Prince of Peace returns to this earth can there be peace—either in the world or the human heart. From now until then it is a fight to the finish. We who are in Christ can have victory, glorious triumph, but only clad in His armor *in the thick of the battle.* The mighty arsenal of Ephesians 6 provides no protection for the back. Those who believe they can win by running away will soon find out how vulnerable they are. May it not take a mortal wound to teach them!

15

Every "Why?" Answered

While some of us here were concerned with holding down a violent case that June of 1971, God handled one in another way in southern Denmark. There, sprawled out on the ground near a gas station on a lonely country road, lay an ex-GI coming off a bad acid trip.

Ken was not asleep—in fact, the speed in Yellow Sunshine makes it impossible for someone who is tripping to sleep. He was no longer communicating with Tony, for he was convinced that his buddy was the devil. He held no hope for the future, for in his deluded daze he felt he had slipped away from earth and was was now in hell. He was utterly without hope; yet he could not turn off his thoughts.

Into this hell God came with all His glory.

First his mind cleared of the compulsive electric-shock *why's*. Then there was an orderly parade before his mind's eye of all the worst things he had ever done. For the first time in his life, he was thinking of these things as *wrong;* this procession of ideas was strangely devoid of all rationalizations and excuses for his behavior. Always before he had assumed he was the way he was because he came from a broken home. Now he seemed to accept the panorama of evil crossing his mind as fact, stark naked, unvarnished, and inexcusable.

He began to wonder *why* again, but this time through a steady stream of quiet logic. *Why did I really drop? Why did I do all those things?*

With these questions came a burning new thought which he had never known before: *I'd like a chance to live life without doing those things. Oh, but all those things—they'd hold me back, keep me here.*

Suddenly from deep inside came a harsh, rumbling cough, which finally spent itself in several moments of violent hacking. It was followed by another one—and another—and another. He lost track of how many of these coughing sessions there were, but he noticed a startling thing. With each period of coughing his head seemed to clear more. Sometimes there would be a period of sniffling instead of coughing, but whatever the physical manifestation, his brain became progressively clearer each time.

A deep conviction came over him that he couldn't kill Tony or himself because something *good* had prevented it. As he lay there, prone on the ground with his eyes closed, he could see the letters *G-O-O-D* spelled out for him. So real was the experience that he reached out his right hand as he saw a hand in his mind's eye reach for one of the *O*'s. He plucked it out and saw the *D* move to the left to close in the word *GOD*.

In that electric moment, the wild wind about him stopped, and there was a perfect calm. Ken got up on his knees, bathed in an ocean of divine peace. Wave upon wave it came, soothing and healing his aching brain, bringing the dawn of a new light in his soul. With this dawn he was lifted up on the inside from every trace of hell and darkness. His chest began to pulsate with a new feeling of well-being and warmth —almost as if an accordion were playing there. He heard nothing, but he knew the music it was playing was an echo from heaven.

Ken realized with great wonder that his mind was now perfectly clear. All of his senses seemed more alive than he ever remembered. He was aware of a conversation going on a few feet away, and he opened his eyes. Two policemen were standing over a mumbling, incoherent Tony.

In a second Ken was on his feet, amazed at his agility and strength. He bounded over to the police, whose faces he could see plainly from the gas station lights.

"What is the problem here?" Ken asked them in a perfectly clear voice. "Can I help?"

"Yes," said the larger of the two in heavily accented English. "Where is your passport? Where are you coming from?"

"From hell," Ken said matter-of-factly as he handed the men his passport.

The two officers chuckled. The tone of the larger one softened as he gave back the passport and turned to leave.

"There's lots of open country here. You'd better move on."

Now Ken got the tent folded up quickly, put the packs on both their backs, and helped Tony get started on their walk. They went only another quarter of a mile before they stopped.

"I can plant our home now before we crash," Ken said, nimbly opening up the tent. This time there was no problem with the pegs. He fitted them into the holes deftly, almost effortlessly, while Tony watched in dazed wonder.

When the tent was up, he dragged Tony inside and got him situated in his sleeping bag before he opened his own. Then he slept, his last conscious thought a *thank you* to the One who had wrought this miracle in his life.

Ken awoke just at dawn. The soundless accordion with the great warmth and peace was still going on the inside. He was glad that Tony was asleep. He wanted to be completely alone with the One who had brought him this great peace and lifted him out of hell.

He slipped out of the tent and caught his breath at the beauty which met his eyes. Could these only be wheat fields shining under a bright sun? Or was this really heaven and all the happiness he felt inside just a glad part of the blessed place?

The colors seemed celestial in their brilliance. Ken had never seen the world through eyes like these. Everywhere, everything he saw was good, filled with beauty. Suddenly he realized his cheeks were wet with tears, but there was no sadness in him. These were tears of joy, an overflow from a heart so filled with love he thought it might burst if it couldn't spill over.

Why, this beauty's always been there, he thought. *I just never noticed it. This is the land of the Creator. You—You're the One who met me last night and took me out of hell. Thank you, God.*

While Ken had been lost in his reverie and discoveries, Tony had waked and walked down to the gas station to get a Coke. Now Ken saw him walking back—clearly in a sour mood. Somehow though, all Ken could feel for Tony was love, a great desire to do good things for him and help him. None of the grouchy or cutting remarks seemed to have any effect on him. This was such a different Ken from the one Tony knew that the swarthy youth often looked over at his blue-eyed, obviously happy companion with real amazement.

At one point when the boys were taking the tent down, Tony hurt himself on one of the tent pegs and swore.

"Jesus Christ!" he said.

Instantly Ken felt a strong reaction of shock with his inner accordion.

"Tony," he said sternly, "if we're going to be friends and take this trip together, you won't say that any more!"

No wonder Tony looks stunned, Ken thought ruefully. *I used to swear like that all the time myself.*

Tony sat, his jaw open in amazement for the next few minutes, while Ken heated a can of beans for them on a Sterno can. As Tony watched his buddy closely, he noticed something very different about him. His eyes seemed to shine, almost to beam light out through them. Tony had never seen anything like this in all his life. Then there was the smile that just wouldn't wear off. What did Ken have to smile about anyway? He had been even more freaked out than Tony, and Tony sure knew how he felt on this morning after. But the weirdest thing of all was when Ken told him this can of beans was the best meal he had ever eaten in all his life. Clearly he had flipped!

"How much water do we have left?" Tony asked glumly, as both boys finished their beans and began to get ready to leave. "Beans really make you thirsty."

Ken looked in the canteen.

"Enough for one of us," he answered. "Here, you take it. I can wait until we get more."

Tony was almost frightened at this remark. Ken had been selfish ever since he had known him. His response before would have been to drain the contents before he answered, and than just announce that there was none left. What kind of flipping was this anyway?

As the boys prepared to start hitchhiking into Copenhagen, Ken picked up the empty bean can and tucked it into his gear. It was the first time he had ever minded littering in all his life, but today even throwing a can along the side of a remote country road was unthinkable to him. *What?* he thought. *Spoil all that beauty? Never!*

After a weary day of walking and no rides, the boys spent the night at a youth hostel. Even the icy cold shower felt good to Ken. Somehow it seemed important to get clean on the outside now that he had been so marvelously cleansed on the inside. He was careful to clean up the shower area before he left it too—an unthinkable thing in his former indifference.

The hostel was situated on the edge of a lovely small lake. Ken could hardly wait to get his clothes on and go down to the water alone. As he walked down to the water's edge, he looked up into the clear, evening sky. A few sea gulls glided overhead, and he found his eyes bathed with tears again. *Thank you for letting me see life through these eyes, God,* he thought. *Now I know why the sea gulls are flying. They're there for the same reason I'm here—for You!*

As Ken sat on a bench on the shore, a little girl and boy walked by, kicking stones and laughing. Inside, Ken's accordion thrilled more and more as he thought of the joy these children were giving *Him*. Then he saw two racing shells on the lake, each with a team of rowers working in perfect harmony. Again he was full of joy just meditating on the way *He* must love their unity in their task.

Ken waited for sunset, to drink in every bit of the beauty God had put into the lake scene. Just loving what he saw and loving the One who made it all seemed to make his accordion thrill more than ever. When it was dark, he strolled into the tiny town nearby.

On his left he saw a pornographic shop. Before, he had shared the opinion of his buddies that these places provided an excellent reason for traveling through Denmark. Now he found himself *flying* to the other side of the street. *I can't take Him in there*, Ken thought. *Now that He's on the inside with me, He and I are so tight I don't want anything to ruin it. I just want this accordion to keep on playing forever.*

The second day in Copenhagen the accordion stopped. *Why?* Ken asked the One who had worked the miracle in his life. *If you're the Creator, and you're all powerful, and you're the One who brought me out of hell; surely you can give me an answer to this one question: Why did it stop?*

Not long after he asked this question, someone handed him a small printed invitation to a coffeehouse in the city.

Why not go? he mused. *About the worst thing that could happen to me is a bad cup of coffee.*

Later he found his way to the coffeehouse and sat down at a table near the door. He was joined by an American girl, Laura, who began to talk to him about Jesus Christ and the change He had made in her life and the lives of her friends.

Ken was not very interested. He had heard this kind of talk before, and he associated it with evangelism campaigns and Bible-banging-fundamentalists. He looked around him and noticed a number of other young men like himself, with bored, amused expressions on their faces, listening to zealous, bright-eyed young people.

Suddenly something Laura said caught his attention however. She was saying that the greatest change she had ever seen in a life was with her German girl friend Gerta, whom she had lived with in Berlin. This girl had formerly lived a very negative life and had a boyfriend who was the same way. After Gerta found Christ, she got a great burden for her boyfriend and began to pray for him night and day. Often Gerta and Laura would pray for him together. However, he would not listen to Gerta and just threw away the letters she wrote him with Bible verses in them.

Ken's heart nearly stopped beating as Laura talked. *He* was that wayward boyfriend; he was the one Gerta had prayed for and written to. He had thought she was such a fool at the time, that he was so clever to see life more clearly than she did.

Laura was saying something about Jesus Christ coming to save Ken from his sin when in a flash he had the answer to his question of the afternoon. The night before he had acted like the old Ken and been out on the town with an unsavory bunch. That's when the accordion stopped. Evidently Jesus Christ was the One who had met Him out on the road that lonely, wild night. Laura was saying He had died for Ken's sin. No wonder He couldn't stand for any more of it in his life!

In that moment it was as if scales fell from Ken's eyes, and the accordion started again on the inside—powerfully, warmly, bathing him in love.

"Laura," he said, his eyes shining, "I was stationed in Berlin; I dated Gerta. I am the one you are talking about."

"Praise God!" Laura said with tears in her eyes, "for this miracle of His."

"It's more of a miracle than you know," Ken said. "This afternoon I prayed to God for an answer; this evening my question has been answered while you were sitting here talking to me. Now I know the name of the One who's found me. It's Jesus!"

Soon several of the workers in the coffeehouse surrounded Ken rejoicing with him in his new-found faith. But he was more concerned about the other conversations he heard going on around him, other lost world travelers giving this theory or that theory in their fight against God. He trembled as he heard the excuses these fellows gave for why they couldn't believe in God. He wanted to scream out to them, "What's wrong with you people! Are you blind?"

Then it hit him. *This is what it's all going to be about,* he thought. *I know what a difficult thing it is going to be to talk about the simple truth—about God—because I know what it means to be blind.*

Six months later Dick and I met Ken in Mayo, Maryland at the home of Ed and Mary Moore, close friends in the Lord. He had just come home from Europe, where he had traveled through fifteen countries with one simple prayer: "Lord, you know I am new in your family; so I need to be with believers. You put me with them."

In all fifteen countries he ended up with Christian families—none of whom he had known before!

The night we met him he had just prayed, "Lord, get me in with the right bunch of believers right away."

We heard his testimony, and it struck me at once that he must have been in the same Youth With a Mission coffeehouse with Marti Smith, Eleanore and Carl's daughter (chapters 9 and 10). When I asked him about it, he grinned at me.

"Sure I remember Marti," he said. "I was baptized with her."

During the course of the evening at Moore's, we had a group deliverance meeting. After an hour or so of seeing the Lord bring about many thrilling deliverances, I walked over to Ken and asked him if he had been freed of any demon powers during the meeting.

"No," he grinned up at me, "but I really do understand what happened to me on the ground that night out in Denmark now. As I watched these people coughing and retching here, it took me right back to that wild night on the Danish country road."

Later that night Ken was baptized in the Holy Spirit, and the glory shone even brighter through those extraordinary blue eyes of his.

The next night we saw him again, and got around to discussing prayer in the Spirit. I explained to him that if we persist with the few syllables in the prayer language, God will often give a far greater fluency and vocabulary in just a few weeks.

Again Ken grinned at me, the Jesus-life radiating from his eyes.

"Maybe the Lord knew it would be hard for me to wait," he said. "I was praying in that new language until five A.M. this morning."

"What about the accordion inside, Ken?" I asked. "Still going?"

"Always," he whispered, a softness blending with the beam coming from his eyes. "Briefly losing it in Copenhagen gave me the fear of displeasing Him. If ever it slows down or eases off inside, I know something's wrong. Then I've got to stop what I'm doing, tell Him I'm sorry, and the accordion starts up again."

Late that night I lay awake thinking of the things God had taught me through this young servant of His.

"Thank you for the Jesus people, Lord," I whispered. "Thank you for this great revival among the young and for the freshness of their experience with You. It's obvious we needed them more than we dream. May the reality of their love relationship with You close the generation gap and help to make eager children of the rest of us, just as tender to the work of Your Spirit within as they are."

16
Snare of Paranoid Schizophrenia

Six months had gone by since the two ex-servicemen freaked out on their bad drug trip in Denmark. Now there was no heavy pack on Tony's back, only an unbearable burden in his mind.

The dingy room in the veterans' hospital was small, decorated only by some faded blue drapes at the dusty windows. Bare pipes, knocking noisily from time to time as the heat came up, ran from floor to ceiling on the left of the window.

Whoever got the bright idea of painting the walls gray? Tony thought. *They must have it in for everyone in this place. It has all the cheerfulness of an old tomb, complete with damp air and mold.*

There was one chair in the room. It had been between the closet and the bed, but Tony had moved it in front of the radiator and window. That way he could look at the door all the time. He had come in through it, and the one hope he had left was that he would one day walk out of it—for good.

The ancient piece of furniture was a Morris chair with musty, well-worn dark green cushions. On its arm Tony kept his best book on astrology. He never wanted that out of his reach, particularly since his mind got so badly blown in Denmark. If he kept casting horoscopes for himself, surely someday he would hit on a plan to get himself out of here, sharp Scorpio that he was.

It was his third night in the hospital. His stomach was churning like an old fashioned ice cream mixer—had been since supper. He felt like he had been on the high seas for several days, but he could not throw up. Something just seemed to keep his dinner lying in there riding the earthquake.

They must have poisoned me or put drugs in the food, he thought. *I was a fool to eat it. I went without food for six days before I got in here; I could have held out a little longer.*

There was a knock at the door.

"May I come in?" a foreign-sounding male voice said.

"Suit yourself, man," Tony answered sullenly.

The pleasant, twinkling eyes of the older man met steely, cold resistance in those that stared at him as he entered the room. He ignored the lack of welcome and, extending his hand in greeting, walked over to the hostile, bearded youth seated in the Morris chair.

"Hello, Tony," he said, finally dropping his right hand since the youth would not return the handshake. "I'm going to be your doctor. My name is Dr. Sikorsky, and I want you to tell me how you feel."

"Awful," Tony snapped. "What did you expect after what they gave me at supper?"

The doctor walked back to the bed and leaned against it, folding his arms on his chest and smiling down at the boy.

"What's the matter? Don't you like our food?" he asked.

"Bag it, man," Tony yelled. "It's not the food; it's what they put in it."

The doctor's kind eyes did not react to Tony's revelation of the crime of the hospital staff. He kept smiling and began to speak very slowly.

"Tony, no one has put anything in your food. You said when you were admitted that you had gone without food for nearly a week. You did not eat that day nor yesterday. Today, I hear you have eaten two big meals—enough to make up for several you lost. You shouldn't have started back on meals that heavily; it's probably made you sick."

"Liar!" Tony shouted at the physician. "Do me a favor and split, will ya?"

Wordlessly, Dr. Sikorsky opened the door and left the room.

That kooky shrink! Tony thought. *Why can't he remember to shut a door behind him?*

He wanted to run and slam it shut so hard it would shake some of the loose plaster from those gray walls. Maybe he'd put his foot through it just to show them how strong he was. Oh, he was strong all right—so strong he could kill that shrink with his bare hands.

No, that wouldn't be the in thing, Tony thought. *If I do that, they might put me in the klink like they just did Al. He was great, talking to me in letters like that. We understood each other, but not one of them could understand us. It was neat.*

Suddenly Tony's head began to pound. Suppose the shrink was telling the truth and they had not drugged his food?

The doctor walked in front of his door on his way to the elevator just as this thought popped into Tony's mind.

"Hey, Doc," Tony called out hoarsely, jumping up from his chair and bounding out of the room in a few giant steps in order to catch up with the older man. "How come you don't think that lousy bunch would put something my food, huh?"

Dr. Sikorsky wheeled around and gave the slender, short youth a long look as they both stopped.

"Because it's not *them* at all, my boy," he said. "It's *you!*" With that, he put his hand on Tony's shoulder for a minute, his eyes kind but unyielding as they locked with the dazed ones set in the face framed by an ill-kempt mane and beard.

Then he turned on his heels and was gone.

Waves of shock settled over Tony as he stumbled back to his room, closed the door, and finally slumped into the sagging Morris chair. His hands shook as he ran them through his black hair.

Wow, I need to comb this mop, he thought. *I guess I've been so uptight I didn't notice how messed up it was.*

Suppose he's right. Suppose it's me, after all. Then I'd have to admit I've been wrong all this time, and that can't be right. I can't be wrong. Or can I?

Tony's body began to shake, as it had so often lately. Then the awful fears of recent weeks began to envelop his mind in a kind of swirling blackness.

I'd better lie down, he thought. *I may black out again. It's not safe up there on the bed, so I'll make me a pad underneath. They won't find me there. I've got to get away from them. They're all out to get me.*

Tony got up and wove his way to the bed as the room pitched and reeled crazily around him. He tore the blanket off the bed, sliding underneath the iron frame and rolling up, cocoon-like, in the cover. He pressed his body right next to the wall at the far side of the bed, his heart beating wildly as he looked back toward the crack of light from the hall which shone under the closed door.

Suddenly a whole roomful of horrible faces began to appear before him. There was the leering Boggs whom he had seen just the week before—the minister who was also a psychic medium, the one who told him he could get help from his dead uncle. There was Mrs. Endor, den mother for all the problem boys in his neighborhood while he was growing up. She tried to help him after he got home from Denmark by practising black and white magic on him. He had been able to talk to her; he liked her. Why was she laughing at him now, with that awful grimace? Then he recognized that smooth talker down at the spiritual center (he couldn't remember his name) whose bag was self-awareness, parapsychology, and Eastern meditation with yoga. Why hadn't it helped? Why had not anything helped?

Sweat began to pour out on Tony's forehead as a whole array of laughing voices began to jeer at him from every corner of the room. Evil, inviting smiles looked down at him from the faces. Tony closed his eyes and began to pound his fists against the floor.

Suddenly the faces changed and they were not human any more. Even with his eyes closed he could still see them. Now they were dwarfish, grotesque gnome-like figures all pointing an accusing finger at him, putting him down.

"God, *help* me!" he cried out.

Just as suddenly as they had appeared, the noises and faces were gone. The pain in his knuckles made him realize that he was still pounding his fists against the floor.

Man, I'd better cool it, Tony thought. *If they find me violent, they'll put me in the klink.*

Slowly he crept out from under the bed, still wrapped in the blanket. Propped on his elbows, he dragged his mummified body to the Morris chair, wearily sliding up into it by using his rubber heels to get the leverage he needed for the push.

At times he dozed. When he awoke, he stared at the door where he had come in. When the first rays of dawn began to steal in the dingy window behind him, Tony never turned around to look out at all. He kept on gazing at the door—a symbol of the freedom he had lost.

He could not get the doctor's words out of his mind. *It's you—It's you—It's you.*

Suddenly a sly, diabolical laugh interrupted Tony's thoughts, and he lurched forward in his chair. *Where did that come from?* he thought, his heart beating wildly. *Was it inside me or outside me? What's so funny?*

"You are," some voice answered him, reading his mind. "You fool! Are you going to listen to what that fellow said when you're a Scorpio and he's a Libra? Yes, you read his zodiac sign right. We haven't let you forget how to do that. After all, we taught you that. Don't disobey us, or you're on a collision course. We're your only friends now. You'll have to listen to us and do exactly what we say—exactly what we say—*exactly what we say.*"

An iron clamp banged shut somewhere in Tony's head as the waves of sound whirred through his ears. A siren shrieked from the hospital emergency entrance, blending with the screaming voices in one fantastic discord. A numb cold began to creep up from his feet and spread through the other parts of his body. He tried to move, but it was already too late. Paralysis had set in leaving one hand weirdly frozen in mid-argument, the thumb and fourth finger rigid.

When Mike opened the door at breakfast time, Tony never saw him. Hostile eyes stared hypnotically toward some scene hidden from the attendant's eyes. A dark, paranoid scowl completed the schizoid trance. A disheveled mane of hair and beard framed the tormented face, accented by the oddly gesturing, corpse-like hand. The grotesque scene Mike confronted looked like the portrait of a medieval sorcerer framed by the window behind the patient.

I'd better get Dr. Sikorsky, Mike thought. *Tony's gone catatonic.*

It was three months later—late summertime now. A steady rain drizzled down outside Tony's window, and occasionally a wet branch would brush against it, sloshing the large maple leaves at the streaks on the glass in a half-hearted attempt to wash them.

Tony's mother sat in the Morris chair; his father leaned against the bed post watching his son who lay on the bed with his hands under his head. Julie had a small sewing kit with her, and she was busily darning some of Tony's socks which had not passed her weekly inspection of his clothes. Her hands shook a little; on the way out she would slip into the ladies' room and get the brandy kept in a cologne bottle in her purse. These visits to Tony in this depressing place were such a strain. Any mother would need some help to calm her nerves after an ordeal like this.

"Son," Roger said, clearing his throat and obviously preparing to make an important announcement. "We've talked to Dr. Sikorsky, your mother and I, and he's willing to give convalescent leave a try, provided you are in our custody at all times. He says the course of shock treatments have improved your condition, and you are responding well now to the tranquilizer they have you on."

"But he also says I'm not well yet. Right?" Tony snapped.

"He says you are *better*, Tony," Roger said carefully. "Look at the bright side for a change, won't you? His choice of the word indicates there has been some improvement."

"Bag it, man," Tony said, waving his arm in a negative gesture at his father. "He's been very frank with me, that guy. He told me he wouldn't let me get out of here at all if he had *all* the say around here, but I kept wanting out and asking higher-ups. The brass just had a meeting and decided anyone who's been stacking up brownie points can go provided they've got family to lock them up."

"Why, Tony," Julie said, her blue eyes opening wide as she looked at her son. "What on earth are 'brownie points?' "

"Staying on good behavior, Mom," the swarthy youth said, sardonically smiling out of one side of his mouth. "The game here is that you don't get rough and get thrown in the klink, you don't hallucinate, and you speak up to everyone who talks to you. That means you're better."

Julie's face blanched in fear. Tony knew what she was thinking. Chicken! She was really afraid to have him home; afraid it wasn't safe.

Roger tapped his foot against the floor, looking down at it first and then over at Julie.

"Son," he said finally, "we've agreed to try it, as Dr. Sikorsky has suggested, as an experiment. If it doesn't work, you'll have to come back. I know you want to leave here, so I believe you will do your best to make it work. Suppose we come for you Friday?"

"Okay," Tony said indifferently, enjoying the discomfort he knew his parents felt at his lack of enthusiasm in being with them again. "But what do you expect me to do all weekend, just sit around and go stir crazy? Man, I gotta have action, or I'm going to split."

Suddenly Julie sat up and smiled brightly as if a new thought of great magnitude had just come to her.

"You *can* do something this weekend, Tony," she said. "Remember your friend Ken from army days, the one you were mustered out with?"

"Sure I remember," Tony said suspiciously, watching every move his mother made. "What's with him?"

"He's helping out in some coffeehouse in the city," Julie said. "He called us last night and asked where you were. He sounded awfully sorry to find out what happened to you after you left him in Copenhagen, and he asked if there were any chance you might get home this weekend. Something about some special rallies and a concert or two somewhere."

Tony sat up on his bed, bracing his arms on its sides to steady himself. He felt dizzy. He didn't really want to see Ken since he knew he'd gotten mixed up with those Jesus freaks in Denmark. Still, anything was better than sitting home with this pair of phonies all weekend, and Ken may have gotten over that bag by now. He might even have some drugs on him.

"Uh, Mom," Tony said nonchalantly, "you can call him and tell him I'll go, I mean being that I'm coming home Friday and all."

"Oh, Tony, that's just great!" Julie said, putting away her sewing and running over to her son's bed to give him a big hug. "I'll invite him back for dinner with us Saturday night. How about that?"

"Suit yourself," Tony said coldly, not responding to her embrace in any way and stiffening himself to endure it.

"Visiting hours are over," a crisp, nasal voice announced over the hospital loudspeaker.

Julie turned abruptly toward the door so that her son would not see the tears which his total rejection of her embrace had brought to her eyes. She put the mended clothes in his bureau and started into the hall without waiting for Roger.

The father shook his son's hand warmly, but it was a wet fish in his hand. A stony, suspicious stare was all the reply his cheerful "Goodbye, son" earned. Roger left the room quickly, got his handkerchief out, and was furiously blowing his nose by the time he caught up with Julie.

They were a striking couple. Roger had always been good looking, and the silver accents at his temples now gave him a dashing, successful appearance. Twelve years had aged Julie very little since the days of watching Tony pitch at Little League games. She was still a very beautiful woman, with her strawberry blond hair piled high on her head in an attractive upsweep. One of the resident interns smiled in frank admiration as he passed her. Julie dropped her eyes, walked a little faster up to the elevator and pushed the *down* button twice.

The couple rode to the first floor without conversation. Roger seemed to be in deep thought; Julie was more nervous than usual, her hands shaking badly as she tried to put on her gloves.

"Where do you think we failed?" Roger said suddenly with uncharacteristic candor.

Julie looked up at him, startled by the remark. Had she heard him aright—*Roger* admitting he might have made a *mistake?* His hurt, pleading eyes convinced Julie that he was serious; he really wanted an answer to his question.

Well, he's asked for it, she thought bitterly; *so he's going to get it!*

"Oh," Julie said casually, with a shrug of her shoulders, "some place between the tax returns and the race to become an executive in the company! I'll meet you at the car; I'm going to stop in the ladies' room for a minute."

17

An Alcoholic's Answer

Julie slipped out of the AA meeting without talking to anybody. She deliberately avoided Myrna and Thelma who were heading for the door where they usually met before going out to coffee together. Instead, she turned around and went out the door near the stage entrance of the auditorium. She did not want to talk to anyone tonight. It might spoil the sense of expectancy which was welling up within her.

The old familiar shaking was back in her hands as she turned the wheel of her car and headed out North Drive toward home. It was nearly two days since she had seen Tony. He had left with Ken after supper Saturday night to spend the night in the city with him and go to the rally and church concert Sunday. She and Roger expected him home Sunday night, but he had called and told them he wanted to stay in town one more day with "these great people."

Julie just couldn't get over that phone call! Tony had sounded so good—so different from any time she remembered in the past four years. His voice seemed clear, and his thoughts were not confused and muddled as they had been.

He told her he was not afraid anymore; he felt at peace. She wondered if she dared to believe him.

It made Julie wince as she thought of Tony with matted, frowsy hair and beard, and a sullen, listless look in his eyes. He hadn't always been that way. What had happened to her Little League baseball pitcher and star performer in the school band concerts? Was it all the drugs, or did the yoga and astrology kicks have something to do with it?

Julie caught her breath when she pulled into the driveway of their lovely split-level home. The light in Tony's room told her he was already there. Would he be better or was this just some cruel joke to dash her hopes on the rocks again?

As she walked into the recreation room from the garage, Julie fumbled in her purse for the cologne bottle. Then she stopped, slammed the bag shut with sudden resolution, and walked upstairs.

No, I'm not going to give in right after an AA meeting, she thought. *If it gets too rough with Tony, I can always take some later.*

As soon as she shut the kitchen door, Julie heard Tony open his own door and start to bound down the stairs, two at a time. As soon as she saw his face at the doorway to the kitchen, she knew it was true. He really *had* changed.

"Hi, Mom," he said with a smile on his face and a radiance in his eyes she had never seen before. But best of all was the voice; it was her son's voice, back for the first time in at least four years.

The shock was too much for Julie. She buried her face in her hands and started to cry. Then, to her amazement, the next thing she knew her son's strong arms were around her, and he was kissing her on the cheek. It was the first time he had kissed her since he left for college.

She pushed back from him a little just to be able to look into his eyes. They were beautiful! No glazed stare, no narrow, hostile slit—just love.

"What happened, darling?" she whispered. "What has come over you?"

Her son took her hand and swung it back and forth playfully, the way he had years ago when he come in from school with some special news. Then he led her over to the breakfast table, and they sat down together.

Julie grabbed both Tony's hands in hers, as her eyes searched his in greater and greater wonder.

"It's not *what* happened to me, Mom," Tony said slowly, "it's *who!*"

"Did you meet some special girl?" Julie asked.

"Oh no, nothing like that," he went on. "I met *Jesus!*"

"Tell me about it," Julie said, bewildered and stunned, but very curious. "Tell me *all* about it like you used to do when you got home from baseball practice, and I'd just sit and listen for hours."

"Okay," Tony said, slouching back in his chair, folding his arms on his chest and grinning at his mother broadly, confidently. "It all began with that first rally Ken took me to Saturday night after we left here. There were some Jesus kids down from a converted barn in upstate New York holding an open air concert and talking to the kids right on the streets down in Whitestone. Some of the Jesus people had real stories to tell. I mean, several had been acid heads, and one fellow told how Jesus had delivered him after he'd been strung out on heroin for seven years. One unmarried girl had had a baby, and another one of the fellows had been in jail. They weren't what you'd call straights, any of them. But they all had one thing in common; like Ken was telling us at supper two nights ago, Jesus had, like, *changed him* so he didn't want the acid any more. They all talked like that.

"After the street rally, we went over to Beechhurst where a minister and his wife lived who were putting up the out-of-town kids. They all had sleeping bags which they spread out all over the floor. We talked all hours of the night, and Ken and I ended up sleeping on the floor there too.

"One of the things I especially remember about that night was one of the girls singing 'Jesus loves me, this I know, accompanying herself on her guitar. That song haunted me all that night.

"The next morning they had a church meeting, out in

Westbury, where they were supposed to give testimonies (that's what they called these stories about the changes in their lives) and sing a few numbers. Well, I tell you I wanted to split; I couldn't see the church bit for anything; but I was with Ken, and he was driving, so I had no choice.

"Bob, the minister we were staying with, was guest speaker. After the kids gave testimonies, he talked about the need to come to Christ and really turned me off. I began to wonder how long this thing would last. I knew the kids had amplifiers in their truck and were planning an outside concert in the churchyard, but I didn't know it was for last *night!* Wow, what on earth was I going to do in the meantime?"

"What did you do?" Julie interrupted. "I can hardly picture you going to church and hanging around afterward! Did Ken take you somewhere?"

"No, that was the worst part," Tony went on, grinning even more broadly as he spoke. "We couldn't split because he had to help the Jesus people set up their amplifying equipment. Also, the people in the church had a big feed for everyone on the lawn; so we had to stay there and eat.

"I got in one of those moods, Mom, while everyone was eating. I didn't feel like eating or talking, and those Jesus kids were trying to make me do both. I could have slugged a couple of them. Also, while we were unloading the truck, the driver was giving some orders that weren't the best way to do it; so I tried to set him straight and he put me down. Wow! All I wanted to do was split from then on. I mean!"

"Then how come you got changed yourself," his mother interjected, "if you were in a mood like that?"

"I'm getting to that. Ken was sort of taking care of me. He kept coming back every few minutes and would get down on his haunches next to my chair and talk to me. But that guy—you know how he likes people—he kept running off to talk to other kids and folks too.

"Finally I noticed him talking to a woman who had come with friends and her two teenage sons. They were from out of town—upstate too, but not the same area as the barn kids.

Ken talked to her a long time, and then he brought her over to meet me.

"Man, this is *a bad scene,* I thought. *I'd better split right now before he sics any churchy dame on me."*

"Was she as bad as you suspected?" Julie asked.

"Well, no. She wasn't exactly *churchy* either; she was different. She didn't mince any words. She told me Ken and the Jesus kids had told her I had demons in me, and Jesus could get them out, if I was only willing."

"The very idea!" Julie said indignantly. "She had some nerve. I didn't know there were still superstitious people around like that."

"Say, Mom," Tony pleaded gently, "please wait till you hear the whole story, okay?"

"Okay," Julie answered, somewhat taken aback.

"That woman, Mrs. Brooks, said to me: 'Tony, we want to help you today, but first of all you've got to come to Jesus as your own Lord and Savior. Have you ever done that?'

" 'I thought I did yesterday,' I told her, 'but then one of these kids turned me off, and the good feeling I was starting to get went away.' "

" 'Well,' Mrs. Brooks said, 'you've got to depend on facts, not feelings anyway. Look here in the Bible with me, in the third chapter of John.' "

Julie was amazed to see Tony get out a small pocket Testament from his jacket and open it for her to the very place he was talking about.

"Where did you get that?" she asked.

"From Ken," Tony answered. "You see how it tells here about a religious kind of bird coming to see Jesus at night, because he was too chicken to get caught with him in the daytime. He wanted to know how to get to heaven, and Jesus told him how. He said, 'You must be born again.' "

"What does that mean?" Julie asked in surprise.

"That's what I asked," Tony said. "Mrs. Brooks said the answer is down in verses 14 and 15. Here, read them for yourself."

" 'And as Moses lifted up the serpent in the wilderness,

even so must the Son of Man be lifted up; that whoever believes may in Him have eternal life,' " Julie read. "What does it mean?"

"Mrs. Brooks told me the answer was over in Numbers 21: 4–9. It's a weird story about the people of Israel getting bitten by snakes, Moses praying for them, and God giving them, like, an antidote. He told Moses to make a brass snake and put it on a pole; then anyone who would just look at it would be cured and live.

"Well, Mrs. Brooks told me there could only be two kinds of people in that camp. She said she'd take one of each to see if I understood it. They were both bitten by the snakes and both lying on their pads in their tents when their folks came in and told them about the brass snake and what God said.

"The first one said, 'Forget it. What I need is some medicine,' but the second one had them take him out right on his pad, to the desert where the brass snake was. He just took a look and he got well. He said something like, 'I don't know how it could work; but if God says so, I'll try it.'

"Then she asked what happened to those two fellows. Wow! If she only know what I was going through while she was talking away like that. My mind was stopping as if it were dead. There was a roaring in my ears so bad I could hardly hear a word she said. That story really blew my mind. The sweat began to pour out on my forehead. I could feel my arms and legs shaking, but I did hear her voice calling out to me, 'Tony, Tony, what was the difference between those two boys?' "

" 'The last one believed God,' I said, and I almost passed out when I said it. I felt like I was going to choke or scream. Mrs. Brooks saw the shape I was in; so she called over that minister I'd stayed with the night before and Ken. She asked me if I could believe God like that—just take a look of faith at Jesus on the cross when He died for my sins. I said I could, and then the action began."

Tony began to sweat again at the temples, remembering the ordeal of the day before.

"The strangest thing happened then, Mom. You probably won't believe it. At first I thought it was a game. My own hands were up around my neck. But then I couldn't get them free, and they got tighter and tighter. Mrs. Brooks didn't say anything to me; she just called some more of the fellows from the Jesus kids to help. They pulled my hands down, and she started to talk to the demons in me, commanding them to speak their names right out and come out of me in Jesus' name.

"I still thought it was a game she was playing until I began to feel the first one slither up through my body and then go out my mouth with a loud yell. I tell you, I didn't make that yell. Something else with a life all its own did. Then I knew this was no game.

"For the next three hours my body was thrashing around, and half the time I didn't even know what was going on. I know I was violent and had to be held down. I know they were commanding demons to come out of me, and something sure was happening when they did. When it was over I felt like a wet noodle, but I felt clean on the inside.

"Before Ken and I went home with Bob, Mrs. Brooks and that minister and a couple of the Jesus people laid hands on me and asked God to baptize me in the Holy Spirit. They told me I would start speaking in a new language I never learned, and I did.

"Mother, that was the cleanest, best I have felt in my whole life. Jesus has delivered me from those demons; He's changed me and given me His Holy Spirit. That's the only reason I wanted to talk to you about these things, Mom. I have an awful confession to make to you. I hated you, Mother, but I want you to know I have forgiven you."

Julie was in tears, flinching from the terrible truth that she had suspected for so long anyway.

"Why, Tony?" she whispered through her sobs. "Why did you hate me?"

"Because I saw you with Hal years ago, that's why," he said evenly and without any bitterness. "I knew what you two were up to, even though Dad didn't. Once I found you in his arms in the dining room when I got home from practice early and once out on the back porch when I went in the kitchen to make a sandwich."

"And the drinking too? You knew about that?" Julie asked her son, for some reason not wanting to spare herself any agony of truth.

"Oh yes, Mom, I know about that," Tony said gently, taking her small, fragile hands in his as she continued to sob convulsively. "Mom, Jesus has shown me my sin was worse than yours. You gotta believe me. Hating you and judging you were worse than anything you ever did. Now I want *you* to forgive *me* for the rotten failure of a son I've been. It's going to be different from now on, with Jesus."

It was several minutes before Julie could compose herself sufficiently to speak. When she finally did, she looked up at her son as if really seeing him for the first time.

"Tony, do you think I can get to know Jesus too?" she asked softly.

"Sure you can, Mom," Tony said, brimming over with a happiness even greater than he had felt when he came to Christ himself, for he had been in such torment at that time. "All you have to do is take that same look of faith, thank Him for dying for your sins, and ask Him to come into your life. He always comes when He's asked."

Julie bowed her head and prayed, "Lord, You know what I am, and my son knows what I am. I've been a rotten failure as a wife, a mother, and a human being. I'm a drunk, Lord. I learned that in AA, but it's been true all these years. I'm a lousy drunk. I ask you to come into my life and clean me up like you have my son, Tony. You're getting the worst end of the bargain, Lord, but if you can make any sense out of this scrap heap of my life, I invite you to do it."

Tony squeezed his mother's tiny hands.

"Thank you, Jesus," he prayed. "Now you'll just have to take care of Dad and the girls. We've got to have a whole Jesus family, now."

Julie squeezed his hands back. Then she smiled up at him

through her tears, withdrew her hands, and opened her purse. Out came the cologne bottle. She handed it to Tony.

"Here. You throw it over there into the garbage bag. You always were the only decent pitcher in the family."

18
Discovering Marriage Outside the Snare

Within one short week of Julie's conversion to Christ, the brandy bottle disappeared from the top shelf of the linen closet. No gallon jug of wine could be found under the sink just behind the garbage can. No telltale breath announced to Roger that another appetizer had preceded the morning orange juice. Best of all, Julie was up and dressed to get his breakfast every day that week.

However the greatest miracle came when Tony moved back home. For five years his parents had seen nothing of him. During the first two he had gone to college. When he had dropped out and gone into the service, he was stationed in Europe for two years. After his discharge, he had wandered in Europe for a few weeks with his buddy Ken and then army medical officers had him shipped home from Germany with the diagnosis of mental illness. His hospitalization in a veterans' hospital fifty miles from their home ended just two weeks after Ken took him along for the weekend with the Jesus kids. So great was the change wrought in his life by God that the doctors dismissed him. Now, after a

month of staying with Ken, he was home again. The prodigal
son, fully fed up with the corn husks of life, was rejoicing
in fellowship with his heavenly Father and determined to be
a son for the first time to his earthly father and mother.

Roger was amazed at the change in his wife and the happy
reunion with his son. Ever since the first afternoon visit with
Tony in the veterans' hospital, he had despaired of ever
seeing his son sane again. The doctors had not offered a
bright prognosis for this paranoid schizophrenic. Tony's
suspicious, condemnatory, hallucinating personality had
been so spilt off from real life that his parents had resigned
themselves to the idea that he would be institutionalized for
the rest of his life. Now he was home and even hoping to
go back to college in the fall.

What was behind all this change puzzled Roger. It was a
great deal more than religion, that was certain. They had
attended church all their lives. What seemed unique about
both Julie and Tony was their great excitement about a person
—Jesus Christ. They talked about Him as if he were right
there in the room with them, and occasionally Roger got the
odd feeling they might be right. After all, something or
someone was responsible for taking the alcohol and gloom
out of his wife and bringing his son back to the world of
reality. Could it be Jesus as they said?

One night Roger went to see a Billy Graham film with
Julie. As he followed the story of the delinquent son and his
preoccupied parents in *The Restless Ones,* he began to identify
powerfully with the father who was more interested in making
money than in spending time with his boy. After the
Camerons got home that night, Roger could not sleep. Over
and over he thought of the times when *he* had not gone to
the ball games, the band concerts, and the open school
nights of his children because of a commitment which involved
economic gain. The love of money had ruled over
him with a clenched fist, but he had never been aware of it
before.

After tossing in bed for about two hours, Roger got up
and began to pace the floor. With great revulsion he sud-

denly realized that one question had been behind almost every decision he made in life: Will it help my career?

On this altar he had sacrificed his wife and his children. In the early years it had been moonlighting; lately it had been the climb to executive status. Suddenly the great achievement of becoming fourth vice-president of his company looked pale and even ugly to him against the backdrop of an alcoholic wife and a drop-out, psychotic son.

Strange that things were now so different when Roger, supposedly the head of this home, had done nothing to help either Julie or Tony. They were giving the credit to Jesus, and he knew they urgently desired him to see things the same way.

Much as this pressure had irritated him, he could not forget the decision of the movie parents; both husband and wife had come to Christ. It did make a lot more sense to have a whole family going one way together, particularly when their previous way had proven a collision course.

The hall clock struck two. Roger felt a strange significance in this simple thing. *Two are better than one,* he thought. *Now that's from the Bible somewhere, but I don't know where. My mother must have told us that when we were children. She used to read the Bible, and I guess she prayed for me. Funny that I've never prayed for myself. I always thought those things we read Sunday morning in the prayer book were enough.*

He stopped pacing. The moonlight shining in through the window had fallen on Julie's face, and he was startled for a moment by her expression. There was peace there. How well he remembered the tormented look which had often characterized her pretty face in the past.

He walked into their master bathroom and turned on the light, looking into the mirror on the medicine cabinet. Now his own face did not have a peaceful expression. If he were objective and honest, he would have to admit that he looked worried, harried, and even a little frightened. Ruefully, he realized that this was the way he usually looked.

Turning off the light, Roger stood in the dark bathroom for a few minutes with his head bowed. Slowly, in a whisper

he began to pray. "Jesus, if you are God as I've always heard
and you are the one who has changed Julie and Tony, *do*
to me. I give up trying to go it my own way in life. It hasn't
worked. I'm willing for your way now."

Suddenly Roger felt light—as though a heavy burden had
been lifted. Then he felt drowsy. He climbed back into bed
and went right off to sleep.

We heard the whole wonderful story when we met Julie
one day on her way home from Montreal. She is of French
Canadian background, and a member of her family had just
died. Having heard much about us from Tony and Ken, she
decided to stop on her way home from the funeral to meet
us. We insisted that she stay overnight with us, particularly
since it was Friday, and we knew she would enjoy the Friday
prayer meeting.

She did! Furthermore, she got some deliverance and was
thrilled to learn that we do not have to settle down to a
lifetime of coexistence with our most unsettling hangups.
Two demons which had long presided over her life were *hate*
and *self-pity.* They left that night with much sobbing and took
with them a chest pain that Julie reported had annoyed and
hindered her all her married life.

Late that night after Dick had gone to bed and the others
had gone home, Julie and I sat up to talk. It was then that
she told me the sad story of her early married life, her affair
with the next door neighbor twelve years before, and her
retreat into alcoholism. Then she spoke of Tony's alienation
and rebellion in his teen years followed by his leaving home
for good.

"Sometimes it seems to me like a dream that Jesus found
all three of us this past year," Julie concluded, looking into
our fireplace at the brightly burning logs. "I'm sure it won't
be long before our two daughters come to Him too. Think
of it—all five of us in the family of God!"

"He surely will do it, Julie," I answered, putting my feet
up on the raised hearth. "You can claim Acts 16:31 for them

and base your prayers on His promise rather than just wishful thinking."

"I know," she added wistfully. "I'm just starting to learn about claiming promises of God by faith. I wonder if it will work for marriage problems."

"Sure it will," I answered softly, pushing a front log further back on the fire. "I should know. We've been through some pretty deep waters, Dick and I. Apart from the Lord Jesus, we'd never even be together today, much less happy."

Julie looked at me thoughtfully, her chin propped on her right arm which rested on the arm of our wing chair.

"How did you get from one way to the other?" she finally asked. "I mean, how did God work it out in your lives so you began to enjoy being married?"

Now it was my turn to look into the fire. I had a choice: I could either adjust my mask and protect my image, or I could be honest. I decided on the latter course. After all, she had been honest with me.

"Well," I said slowly. "It didn't happen all at once. In my case, coming to know Jesus didn't affect my attitude toward Dick too much. I sort of figured we'd both made a mistake, and the best thing we could hope for was grace to bear it a little better."

A vigorous nod and tears in Julie's eyes told me we were on common ground.

"I had the notion for many years that love was something that just happened; either you had it or you didn't. If you had it, that was great. If you didn't—well, tough. You made your bed, and you'd better lie in it if you were a biblical Christian."

"Isn't that true, Pat?" Julie asked, earnestly looking into my eyes. She had moved forward in her chair and now had both elbows on her knees with her face cupped in both hands. "I mean—I've got to be truthful—that's the way I feel right now."

"The trouble with that kind of reasoning," I said carefully, "is that we are *not* living according to Scripture in that frame of mind. One of the biggest revelations I ever had was an understanding of what Jesus meant when He said, 'A new commandment I give to you, that you love one another, even as I have loved you.' It's a *commandment* to love. The solution for lack of love lies in the *will*, not in the feelings. In other words I can love anyone I decide to love, because it's the Jesus-nature to love.

"What the other person is like has nothing to do with God's kind of love. The Bible says 'while we were yet sinners, Christ died for us.' I think that means there was precious little in our attitude or behavior that made us worth saving, but Jesus still went to the cross and died for us. This tells more about Him than it does about us. It tells us that He loves us because He is love; He can't help but love. If we allow His love to rule in our lives, we can do the same thing. We can will to love those we have no particular reason to love or are not attracted to. As soon as we decide to do it and act accordingly, we discover God is right there with His love to make it real."

"This is really a new idea to me, Pat," Julie said thoughtfully. "Do you mean you can will to love someone you never really fell in love with?"

"No, more than that. I mean you can end up with something even *better* than you have by 'falling in love' when you will to love. If you fall in love, it stands to reason you can also fall out of love. That's the problem with a lot of people's marriages today. They've fallen out of love and think that's the end. They don't realize they are at the point of redemption in their marriage. Here's where the adventure of willing to love begins."

"My, this is really different than what I expected as an answer, Pat. I have been praying for God to give me love for Roger, but I admit I haven't seen much result from that praying."

"Of course not, Julie. You see, you were asking God to do what He's told you to do. This is one of the commonest errors in the Christian life. It's the reason Christians refuse to take authority and cast out demons too. We expect God to do it for us; yet he has made it perfectly clear that His followers are to cast out the demons. No wonder there is so little action when we ask Him to do it for us."

"Then it seems to me the whole thing boils down to obedience," Julie said excitedly. "Here I am, like a spoiled brat, yammering at God to give me the right feelings, and He's been waiting for me to start doing the right things."

"That's right!" I grinned back at her. "Incidentally, there are a couple of books that shed light on the path back to God's way too. They surely helped me. One of them is Larry Christensen's *The Christian Family* published by Bethany Fellowship; the other one is Helen Andeline's *Fascinating Womanhood* published by Pacific Press. Try what they say, and let me know how you come out."

Four months later Julie and I had a chance to go out to lunch together while I was visiting friends on Long Island. I rejoiced to hear how God was working in the Cameron family. She and Roger were going through the Scripture together, and one of their college daughters had come to Christ. Tony was having some real problems, but when she told me how deeply involved he had been in drugs and the occult before he came to Christ, it was understandable.

The waiter had just brought our lemon chiffon pie when Julie blurted out the main thing that was bothering her.

"Pat, how can I really love Roger like I'm supposed to when I can't stand having him make love to me?" she said, dropping two heaping spoonfuls of sugar into her coffee.

"What's the matter with his lovemaking?" I asked quietly, holding my cup of tea in my hands for a minute before I took a sip. The air conditioning was very cold and the hot pottery felt good in my icy hands.

"Oh, he's so rough and awkward at it, he makes me sick," she said in disgust, stirring her coffee with vigorous strokes expressive of the resentment she felt.

"Have you ever taught him how to do it the way you'd like it?" I asked.

"Why, no!" she said in surprise.

"Well, how else is he ever going to learn?" I asked. "You are the one he's trying to please. If you don't communicate to him what pleases you, then he never knows how to improve. That's a good way to keep the frustration level pretty high."

"What makes you think he's trying to please me?" Julie retorted bitterly. "As long as he gets his kick out of it, everything's all right."

"That's not true," I said, sipping my tea slowly. "There are two sides to sex fulfillment as far as a man is concerned. One side is his own satisfaction in the act. However, even more important as far as his manly self-image is concerned, is his ability to satisfy his wife. If he gets the notion that he cannot do that, he may suffer terrific feelings of inadequacy."

Julie looked stunned for a minute. She took a big gulp of coffee, her face reddened, and she looked down as she spoke.

"Then I guess I'm not the big bargain of a wife I always thought I've been. I've never depended on Roger to bring me to climax. An old itch or scratch was better than his puny efforts. However, since my affair with Hal ended, I have depended mostly on sexual dreams."

"Julie," I said very matter-of-factly, "the source of that kind of satisfaction is demonic. Do you want to carry on your sex life with evil spirits?"

"No! Certainly not," Julie said, recoiling in horror as her face grew pale. "I—I guess I just never realized this was wrong. How do I break this habit pattern?"

"Well for a starter, why not line up your will with the will of God? That's the only way you can get rid of the demonic element permanently anyway. How about deciding—and verbalizing—that from this day forth, you will not get any other sex satisfaction apart from that within your own marriage?"

Julie looked up at me, startled at this apparently revolutionary idea. She picked up her coffee cup and drained its contents; then she shoved it into the center of the table.

Propping her chin on her elbows, she closed her eyes and prayed silently.

"I just did that," she said. "Now how do I make sure I get rid of all the demonic spirits that have brought me these other experiences?"

"You tell them off in the name of the Lord Jesus Christ," I said.

"All right," Julie said with real determination. "You tell me what to say, and I'll repeat after you."

"Okay, here goes," I said softly. "Satan, in the name of Jesus Christ I take back all the ground I ever gave you in sexual dreams, masturbation, and adultery."

She whispered the words quickly and was soon saying these other things after me: "I refuse, resist, and reject any sexual satisfaction outside my marriage relationship with Roger, and I command every evil spirit responsible for those experiences to depart from me forever. In Jesus' name."

We sat quietly for a minute. I suggested we both silently pray God would reveal any further blocks standing between her and a normal relationship with Roger; then she could confess them as sin and take back from the adversary any ground she had given to him.

As we prayed I had a word of wisdom from the Lord that something unconfessed and deeply disturbing from her youth needed to be dealt with. I asked her if she knew what it might be.

"Yes, there is something," Julie whispered with great anguish. "God is bringing it back to my mind now as you speak. When I was thirteen I was deeply attracted to my mother's younger brother, who was wildly in love with me. He was seventeen when we went on a big family beach party. Afterward we took a shower together—still in our bathing suits, of course—and he kissed me passionately. From that day on there was an aching bond between us. Every time he saw me in the five years or so after that, I could see terrific longing for me in his eyes, and for my part, I was very deeply attracted to him. I've never talked about this to anyone. But now that it's out in the open I think this feeling that what

I wanted was out of reach, out of bounds, has been at the root of my whole strange thinking about love."

As Julie was talking, the Lord was pouring his insight and light onto this situation. Without a trace of hesitation and much surprised at what was coming out of my own mouth, I could hear myself saying, "Julie, a spirit of *incest* entered on the day of the swimming party through the deep tie you felt for your uncle. Renounce it now in the name of Jesus. Take the ground back you gave Satan in that relationship and break the demonic subjection to your young uncle."

Even before she finished praying Julie's whole body began to shudder.

"Demon of *incest*, come out of her in the name of the Lord Jesus Christ," I said in a whisper, fervently praying it would not come out with a scream right there in the restaurant!

After a couple of minutes of shaking all over, Julie sighed deeply.

"It's gone," she said in real wonder. "Oh, Pat, I'm free! I just know it. Thank you so much."

"Don't thank me. Thank Jesus!" I assured her quickly. "He delivered you. I didn't do a blessed thing. In fact when he gave me that word of knowledge about the spirit of *incest* and the steps you needed to take to be free from it, I was floored at what came out of my own mouth. I didn't know any of that!"

"Oh, Pat, isn't Jesus wonderful?" Julie said, jumping to her feet and grabbing the check from the table. "Let's go home. I can't wait to see Roger now. I know it's going to be different."

"It will surely be different all right," I said grinning at her as I got up and made our way out to the parking lot. "But can you imagine how far we would have gone in this complex problem without the power and gifts of the Holy Spirit? To think that people say the spiritual gifts aren't needed today!"

Three weeks later Julie phoned me long distance to tell me her thrilling news.

"Pat, it's like a miracle. All the pain and dread I've experienced in marital intercourse are gone—vanished just like a dream."

"How about the sexual dreams? Are they gone, too?" I asked.

"They sure are," she answered warmly. "What's more, Roger and I are having a real honeymoon together. Everyday I get up and thank God for giving me this man as my husband."

"That's quite a change, Julie," I said. "What happened between you to bring this about?"

"Well, I've been teaching him the kind of lovemaking I like as you suggested. In the beginning I just took his hand and guided him in caressing me the right way. Then I've also been admiring him and letting him be the big man of the family like I guess he always wanted to be. I'll say, 'I never could have opened this can,' or 'I can't get this window open. I just don't have the strength. You do it.' He seems to love to show me how big and manly he is and how able to take care of me."

"Praise Jesus," I said softly. "Your home is coming into divine order fast. How about Roger? Any major breakthroughs in his own life yet?"

"Oh yes, Pat. In a way that's the most exciting story of all. God dealt with me about confessing all that mess with Hal to him; so I did. At first he was just furious, but the truth did set him free just as Scripture says. That iron reserve was broken down by the emotional storm going on inside, which apparently caused the demons *he* had to kick up and come to the surface. I played the Basham tape on deliverance for him, and we had our own private little deliverance service. He got delivered of the *hate, violence, jealousy* and *murder* spirits, and I tell you, he's a new man now. But the strange thing is that he's been much more in love with me than ever before."

"Oh, it's not at all strange," I said. "Before, he was bound. Now Jesus has set him free to love. How about his relationship with Tony?"

"One of the demons Roger was delivered from was the spirit of the *love of gain.* I think the biggest change since then has come in his talks with Tony. Roger always made a big thing of having Tony work his way through college, said it would make a man of him. Well, Tony's job in college was playing trombone in a band where the leader was a drug addict and pusher. All Tony's job did for him was to get him hooked on drugs. He dropped out at the end of his sophomore year and joined the army.

"Now Roger says he wants to send Tony to college in the fall if his mind is really healthy enough to study again. We want Tony to improve before he goes though. He does have days when he's quite hostile and negative despite the fact that he's trusting Jesus. He seems to have a problem keeping the demons out after they are cast out. Do you know why that would be?"

"Well, one reason is because he was so deeply involved in the occult. Such people always face a struggle standing against Satan," I answered. "However, the Lord can unlock Tony's situation as surely as He did yours. We'll be glad to have him come see us if he wants to."

"Okay," Julie said. "I'll tell him. I guess the fault couldn't be on God's side, could it?"

"That's right, Julie," I concluded. "The fault is never on the Lord's side. He can do anything but fail. He's never made a mistake before, and He's not likely to start with Tony."

19
Further Unraveling of the Schizoid Snare

Eleven-thirty one night about a month after I got back from Long Island, the phone rang shrilly, rudely interrupting our first few moments of sleep.

"Mrs. Brooks, it's Tony," the voice at the other end of the wire said. He sounded defiant, but pleading for help at the same time. "Why didn't I stay free after that time when you were here?"

"I told you it would be a battle," my voice said wearily. "Have you been keeping up the fight?"

"Sometimes yes, sometimes no," Tony said a little more softly. "It's hard. There's one demon that I can't seem to get rid of. It was named that day when you were here, but I don't think it came out."

"Which one is that, Tony?" I asked, flicking on the light beside the bed.

"The demon *pride*," he said in a resigned tone of voice. "This one is the big thing. I feel if I can get rid of this, the rest of them will leave me alone."

"It was the ruler demon, Tony," I said. "I knew that when

189

I saw you, but I wasn't sure that it came out. Did you really want it to come out?"

"I don't know. I thought I did," he said reluctantly, "but I went downhill just a few days after you left. I felt really bad the following Sunday when that pastor and his family took me back to the church. I couldn't sit there and listen to the sermon. I got up and started walking up and down in the church telling those hypocrites off."

"That sounds like *pride* all right," I said quietly. "That's not the way to get rid of it, Tony."

"But it's been telling me awful things, Mrs. Brooks."

"Oh, I don't doubt that. They'll feed you lies as long as you will listen."

"They told me if I went back to playing the trombone all my teeth would fall out, and my hair would fall out if I kept going around with these Christians. What do you think of that?"

"That they are lies," I said quietly. "Now which are you going to believe, the lies of the enemy or the Word of God?"

"I want to believe God," Tony said, "but I seem to be chained in these things. It is like there is some, great invisible hold on me, that just won't let me go. The minister and his wife tried to help me. I've spent a lot of time down at their house, but it always ends up the same way. They turn me off, and I get mad and split."

"They are really fond of you," I tried to assure him. "These people love you. They've written me letters about you. They're trying to help you. Why do you keep turning on them like that?"

"I don't know," Tony said, his voice breaking. "Can I come up to see you people?"

"By all means come up, Tony," I said. "Only be prepared for us to tell you some things that may be hard too. Facing truth *is* hard when you've been held by deceptions for so long, but it's only the truth that will set you free."

"I'm coming," he said with a sudden decisiveness. "How about next Friday?"

"That'll be fine," I said.

Lord, help us to be able to help this troubled boy, I prayed. *We don't know the answers, but you do. Show us or him what ground these evil powers still have in his life, on what basis they still keep a hold on Tony. If he's ever going to be completely free, Lord, you know that he'll have to take the rug out from under the enemy and give him no place to stand on in his life. You have to show us that, Lord. We don't know anything. Without you we can do nothing.*

A wonderful peace settled over me as I turned out the light. There was a deep assurance that everything would be all right. The Shepherd is far more concerned for the sheep than we are. He'll have every one safe within His fold, and He knows just how to get them there.

Supper was over. Tony and I were having a talk in the family room. It was a Saturday night, and he had been with us for just one day. The night before our New Testament Fellowship had prayed for the healing of his mind and memories, and he became somewhat more relaxed. He seemed a little better than when he first came, but he was still hostile and tense.

One of my teenage sons was out baby sitting; the other was playing the piano in the living room on the other side of the house. Dick had just gone upstairs to take a shower, when the phone rang. I went to answer it and was jolted by an obscene phone call. After I got back to the family room, I noticed a marked change for the worse in Tony. Something I had just said had evidently turned him off, and an evil look of inexpressible hatred crossed his face.

"Tony, what's the matter?" I asked.

There was no answer. The eyes pierced mine with a strangely hypnotic stare, and I suddenly realized the boy's personality was entirely submerged.

"I'm going to get Dick, Tony," I told him. "We'll be back together in a couple of minutes."

Little did I know of the earthquake going on inside that swarthy, handsome young man. About five minutes before, a wicked but familiar voice had whispered to him, *"I really brought you up here to kill her. I've got it all set up. In a minute or two she's going to get a phone call which I have prepared. Her husband is in the shower; he can't help. Her son is playing the piano loudly and he'll never hear. I have given you a supernatural strength, and you can kill her in a flash as soon as she comes back from that phone."*

Just as I got up to leave and go find Dick, the troubled boy planned to follow the suggestion. However at that moment, a strange thing happened to him. He became completely paralyzed and found himself in a catatonic state. In that moment Tony realized that God had protected me, that he and the demons could not touch me for their evil purpose. He told us later it did more for his faith than all the sermons he had heard since his conversion four months before. A God that real, who could protect His child that surely, could even bring him out of the last tangles of the vicious snare which had so often eclipsed his reason.

Dick and I came back with Charlie and tried to talk with Tony, but all our efforts were fruitless. The catatonic state persisted. Dick took authority over the demons, but they did not respond to us. All we could do that night was put Tony to bed and bind the spirits until morning, trusting the Lord that we could have the human personality of the boy to deal with then.

I tossed for many hours that night. Why had we been unable to help Tony? Why hadn't the demons responded when we addressed them in the name of Jesus? These questions went over and over in my mind, and finally I got the assurance of an answer. It seemed the Lord was showing me that Tony had given his own human will over to the demons; therefore we could do nothing for him until he repented of it.

The next morning was rough going. Our Fellowship meets in our home, and they would be coming whether Tony was aware of what was going on and agreeable or not. We could talk to him, but he was still very sullen and hostile. Dick got him dressed and managed to get him into the service with us, but he got very little out of it.

A brother in the Lord bound the *schizophrenic* spirit in him before the group left. Immediately there was a dramatic change. He began to take an interest in the things about him once more, and even spoke to two or three of the group.

On Monday evening when Dick and the boys were all here, we cast out the demons causing Tony's psychotic problem. There were *schizophrenia, madness, stupidity, epilepsy,* a *mongoloid* spirit, and one that called itself *Yoga.* The manifestations of some of these were classic. The *mongoloid* spirit threw his body about in the same way children move who are extreme victims of mongolism, and it made idiotic, wailing noises in steady crescendo until it left. The *Yoga* demon, with rapid slithering motions, got both his arms and his legs up in the air in incredible positions. There they stayed in perfect balance as his head moved rapidly from side to side, jutting out at a grotesque angle from his neck until the spirit left.

During the week that he spent with us, we urged Tony to tell us his whole story. We knew it would help him to get out into the light those things which were still providing ground for satanic deception; we also believed his story might help a multitude of young people. As Tony shared his experience with us, different demons would rise to the surface of his personality, and he would deal with them himself, right then. We did very little for him in the matter of deliverance that week. I pointed this out to him.

"Tony," I said one morning, "for all your torment, you have made real improvement in the last few months."

"What do you mean?" he asked in amazement.

"The last time I saw you, *we* cast all the spirits out of you," I explained. "Now you are taking authority over many of them yourself and casting them out. Don't you see the difference?"

"Yes, I guess I do," he grinned sheepishly. "You mean even though I'm having a battle still, at least I'm often in charge of it myself?"

"Yes, that's exactly what I mean," I said. "Now tell me about those turbulent college years and why you dropped out and joined the service. What happened to blow your mind so badly that you ended up in the hospital?"

"I think it was my second year at NYU that I got so fouled

up," he said. "I joined a band and started making a little money, getting help from a trombone teacher who was really strung out on drugs. Stan talked me into smoking pot by telling me since I'd be on drugs for sure sooner or later, I might as well learn from someone who really knew what he was doing.

"I should have realized that this guy was no good because he made such a mess of his own life. His wife and children had left him, and he was involved in every kind of freaky thing, but I listened to him and I got mixed up with a bad crowd."

"Did you just stay with marijuana?" I asked.

"No. When I had an accident that totaled my car, I had a bad concussion. Wow, did my head hurt. Before long I was using hashish, and finally I got into sprayed weed. I didn't get on the acid until I dropped out of school and joined the army."

"How old were you then, Tony?" I asked.

"Nineteen," he answered. "I was a sophomore. That was the year I picked up the book on astrology and began to get into it really deep. It was weird, but I found out this was where the big kicks were. Before long I could look at someone and tell what sign of the zodiac they were born under.

"By spring of that year I wanted to split the whole drug mess. Man, that was a bad scene, and I was getting uptight from it. I had to get loose somehow; so I got into Yoga and Eastern religions. I learned to hypnotize myself, and I could cop out anytime I wanted.

"By the time school was out, I had cast a horoscope for myself that showed I'd be in real trouble if I stayed in school. My only favorable move looked like a trip to Europe, so I joined the army and hoped for the best. Sure enough, my division went to Germany. It was there I met Ken and began to drop acid. That stuff really blew my mind. Think of all the traffic with demons I was already in on with astrology and yoga!

"When Ken and I mustered out, we decided to bum our way across Europe dropping acid all the way. Then we each had a bad trip that time on our way to Copenhagen; you know what happened to him there."

"I sure do, Tony," I interrupted. "How come you left him then?"

"Wow, you've gotta be kidding," Tony said. "I thought he'd freaked out for good, with that Jesus game. That's what I thought it was. I split to Germany, freaked out again on a real bad acid trip, and landed in the army hospital. The shrink out there sent me back to the vet hospital near home. The shrinks there diagnosed me as paranoid schiz and told my father I might be there all my life.

"I was there four months before I got weekend privileges. It was on the very first one out that Ken found me at home and took me off to the Jesus rally. Think of that! The next day I met Jesus, and you and those Jesus kids cast all those demons out of me.

"Sometimes I still can't get over it when I think of it. I mean, wow! Ken played that buddy game so well he actually went on a search to find me like that."

"Tony, why do you keep calling everything a game?" I asked. "I've noticed you use that comment over and over again, as if everything in life were a game."

"Well, isn't it?" he asked. "That's what I really thought even when you started casting demons out of me down there last August."

"What made you change your mind?" I asked.

Tony sat quietly reflecting on this matter for several minutes.

"The revolution that went on inside, and the fact that they came out," he said.

"Tony, do you see now that everything connected with the Lord Jesus Christ and His Word is no game; it's really true?"

"Wow, I want to believe that. Yes, I do want to believe that, but it's hard. It's like there's something in me saying, 'It's all a lie. This is just a game too.' "

"That something in you that thinks this is all a game has got to come out, Tony," I said.

"I know you're right," Tony said, putting his hands up to

his head and shaking it back and forth, "but I seem to be afraid to get right down to this one. Something keeps telling me that the deliverance for this will be so violent I won't be able to take it. I'll die in the middle of all that."

"More lies," I said disgustedly. "Why listen to them any more?"

Tony's face changed. The dark paranoid scowl was back, and he faced me angrily.

"Why listen to you for that matter? You've really turned me off a lot since I've been here," he said.

"How come, Tony?" I asked.

"You're always putting me down, right?" he said.

"What are you thinking of specifically, Tony?" I asked.

"Well, like this morning, for instance. We were driving down the Northway. You missed your turn when you had that carload of people to go to the meeting. You blamed me for that, right?"

"Wrong," I said. "That's just not true. I was the one to blame for not making that turn, and I said so."

Suddenly I sensed that the moment of truth for Tony had come. I saw that if Tony could see this little situation as it really had been, he might turn the corner from a life of receiving deceptive impressions from other people into receiving truthful, fair ones.

"But you said it three or four times, and I think you expected me to know different since I drove down to that same place yesterday," he said suspiciously.

"No. That's just not true," I said. "The reason I repeated myself was that I wanted to make sure you understood that I was not blaming you. I did *not* want you to think we were putting you down."

"Then that other woman sitting next to me—she put me down, right?" Tony asked desperately, leaning forward in his chair. His face was contorting in a terrible struggle between reality and the paranoid reaction of a decade.

"Wrong!" I went on doggedly. "She did not put you down. She did the very opposite. She tried to show you love and build you up, but you rejected her."

Suddenly a look of real fear crossed over Tony's face. I knew the truth was beginning to dawn on his soul, and with great rejoicing I moved in on him with the whole thing that God had been showing me the past few days.

"Tony, that's your basic problem; don't you see it? When people begin to show you love, you are afraid to accept it. You turn on them in a paranoid, suspicious rejection of their love. This is what you did with that dear minister and his wife near your home who have been trying to help you all these months. This is what you did with the family who had the prayer meeting down your way. Basically that's what you've been doing with Dick and me and the others all this week as we've been trying to help you. Now isn't that true?"

Tony's lower lip began to quiver, and his eyes filled up with tears.

"How can I guard against this when it starts to happen?" he asked. "Suppose you're right. Suppose this is the reason I'm not really free. How can I stop it from happening?"

"I'll give you one little, simple rule," I said. "Just remember this: whatever causes me to turn against my brother or respond to him in anything but love is not of God; it is from an evil source. Isn't that easy?"

There was no answer now. Tony was sobbing—softly, steadily, redemptively. As the waves of truth hit his consciousness, those honest tears washed layers of deception from his long tormented mind.

"That's what you've done to your father and mother, isn't it, Tony?" I said. "Don't you turn them off whenever they try to help you? Maybe they don't understand you too well, but the way you react to their attempts to help you is what's keeping you bound."

"Yes, I think that's true," he sobbed. "Maybe that's why my younger sister hasn't come to know Jesus yet. Even though she's seen some change in me, she's not seen any change in my basic reaction to her, and that's what counts."

"Tony," I went on quietly. "I want to share with you something that a dear man of God shared with Dick and me several years ago when we were rookie missionaries in

Africa. This fellow had just lost his wife a few days before. We took him on a picnic hoping to cheer him up and divert his mind from his troubles. However it turned out, as it often does in life, that he ended up helping us instead.

"At that time Dick and I were teaching in a mission secondary school. The African students were very rebellious that week and had even staged a one-day walkout. It was upsetting to us, and we didn't know how to handle it. Dick asked this older missionary, 'How do you react when the students reject you and treat you like that?'

"I'll never forget that older missionary's answer. 'Brother, you don't react.' he said."

Tony sat very quietly for a few minutes, the sobbing subsiding as he looked up at me slowly, a beautiful light dawning on his face.

"I think I'm beginning to see it now," he said. "It's only as I'm willing to receive love that I can give love myself. It's only as I stop reacting to *people* and start acting on the basis of Jesus' love for me that I can be a whole person. Is that it?"

My own eyes filled up with tears. "The Lord wants to use you as a channel of His love, Tony, to a multitude of young people who are still just as mixed up as you were. There are many who haven't seen the way out yet. If you can do this, you are going to be used of Him in a mighty way. I just know it."

"I can do it," he said jumping up. "I can do all things through Christ who gives me strength. Now I'm ready to start planning on going back to school, only this time it will be a Christian school. I want to learn the Word and start getting out and working for Jesus. Wow! There's not much time left until He returns, right?"

"Right," I said grinning broadly. "Right on!"

20

Anesthetic of Our Age, the Decimated Gospel

My eyes were opened to the tragic blindness of professing Christians by an experience like that of the Scottish poet Robert Burns in his poem, "To a Louse." Remember his fascination with a small insect's activity on the head of one of the faithful, sitting in front of him in church? Remember her pride and propriety, her utter self-confidence and unawareness? How could anyone forget the poet's profound conclusion to the whole incident:

> "O wad some Pow'r the giftie gie us
> To see oursel's as others see us!
> It wad frae mony a blunder free us
> An' foolish notion.*

One night my husband and I sat in the back of a large auditorium listening to a powerful speaker. As he described the present movement of the Holy Spirit—the return of miracles through believers all over the world—my eyes were

---

* Permission granted to reprint from Oxford University Press.

suddenly distracted from him to two people seated a few rows in front of us. While all other heads in the audience were glued forward, this pair seemed strangely inappropriate. Each remark of the speaker brought exchanged looks between them, varying from outright ridicule to withering scorn.

As my eyes riveted to the strange scene, my mind alternated between a strange fascination and horror. I recognized these people, a mother and her married son. I knew that the man's young wife was at home with their two babies and had prayed that her husband and mother-in-law might come to this meeting. A year before, the desperate wife had nearly committed suicide and had come to us for help. This sneering, self-assured young man was a homosexual who visited gay bars at least twice a week. He was also an accomplished hypocrite active in a prominent evangelical church as well as in several Christian organizations in the area.

The extraordinary thing about the auditorium incident was the attitude of the mother. She knew of her son's moral condition, and she also professed to know Christ as her Savior; yet she had stedfastly resisted the idea that Christians could have demons or that miraculous ministries were needed in our age. She had slandered me widely in her church.

Like many professing Christians today, this woman explained all problems and aberrations of behavior on the basis of modern psychology. Doubtless this was what amazed me most of all. Since psychologists blame homosexuality on excessive "smother love" more than any other one factor, how could this woman have an attitude like that? Where was the sorrow over her own sin and failure in her son's life? Why was there no seeking for an answer from God with whom all things are possible? How could she ridicule the power of the Holy Spirit who offered the only hope for this tormented son's deliverance?

As I sat there stunned by the irony of the little drama, I began to develop a profound loathing for an orthodoxy which shuts out God's power. The words of Dr. G. Allen Fleece, from our days at Columbia Bible College, began to drift through my mind: "Who is so deceived as he that is self-deceived?" He had gone on to explain that the Greek New Testament word for hypocrite meant just that. The Pharisees really deceived no one but themselves; the common people knew them for exactly what they were.

My mind went back over our missionary years in Africa. Had we known Jesus as Deliverer, Healer, and Baptizer in the Holy Spirit as well as Savior, we would never have left the converts we made as weak and uninstructed as they were to meet the great trials of life. If Christ's authority were taken over the evil forces, national churches and mission societies might not have the strife and divisions they do today. Freed from the decimated gospel they have been taught to believe, missionaries would then teach all that He commanded as stated clearly in great commission. Soldiers of the cross, clad in the *whole* armor of God, they would then be victors instead of the victims they so often are.

In those few moments in the crowded auditorium, God gave me courage to dream of a day that is coming—a day when multitudes of His people are "the head, and not the tail," when everywhere they go it will be the norm to have the Lord working with them confirming the Word with signs following. "And in that day," said Jesus, "you will ask me no question." No more doubts in that day! "Until now you have asked for nothing in My name; ask, and you will receive, that your joy may be made full."

Why do your people reject your power, Lord? I asked as the stirring message on His mighty working came to a close. In my mind's eye, He took me back to another day at Columbia Bible College and a Greek class. The professor was greatly upset by a letter he had received from a former student, and he felt led to share it with us. It seems that the student had sought the experience of speaking in tongues one night in a Pentecostal church in Chicago. He stayed long after others had gone, agonizing on the floor with God and pleading for this gift. Suddenly a bright light seemed to flash, an electric shock seemed to go over him, and he found himself speaking in another language.

In the months that followed this experience, this unfortunate young man lost all enthusiasm for the things of Christ. The Word of God became dull and meaningless to him, and he ceased to speak to others about Jesus. For two years he wandered in that wilderness, which ended only when he repented of the whole experience.

As I reflected over this account with the light I now had, it seemed to be a classic case of demon entrance. When I was a teenager, I had been much worse off when the nocturnal breathings close to my ear stopped as I had prayed they would, because they came inside; so this man had gone into darkness when a power outside him had taken over inside bypassing his human will altogether in the process. The key to understanding such a counterfeit experience (one which has been repeated thousands of times over) is that this power worked *instead* of his human will, not through it.

God never bypasses the human will. His original decision to create man with freedom of choice has not been changed. His great risk, as well as His deep joy, lies in our understanding of this truth. Will man choose Him or reject Him? Paradoxically, only when we yield to Jesus Christ as Lord can we ever become completely *free*. The marionette strings of evil power are only finally cut for the bondslaves of Christ; wanderers through an amusement-park Christianity may well find themselves at the end of the day with nothing but a torn stub to show for their ride.

When "accepting Christ" amounts to little more than "voting for Jesus," it is not the salvation of the New Testament. Biblical conversion saves the whole man, not only his soul. It is not just pie in the sky for the by-and-by; it is an adventure with God in the *now* of your life, through a deep love relationship with His Son, in the power of His Spirit.

The words of Jesus to the hopeless, lifetime cripple ring down through the ages in all their penetrating, mask-stripping honesty: *"Do you wish to get well?"* What do you *really* want anyway? Is it a ticket on the golden jet line—or a clean break with the world ties which reduced Lot's wife to a pillar of salt? Is it healing of the body—or a deep, inclusive healing of body, soul, and spirit which requires all the strength and responsibility your illness might excuse you from? Is it freedom from some fear or sex torment—or removal of the very ground on which the demons have preyed?

No matter how blind or stubborn your family, are you willing for God to start some spiritual surgery in *you?* With what ruler spirit are you wrestling?

Could it be that the faults of others occupy your thoughts so fully that you have never given this possibility a thought? Or perhaps your own secret thoughts convince you that you are the only one capable of judging a situation fairly? Such notions are a dangerous delusion. Neither fallen man nor redeemed man is infallible. To believe that we are is *pride,* the thing that brought about the downfall of the shining one who mutinied against God.

Would the loss of your complaints rob your thought life and silence your conversation? Is a mirror a place for sympathy with your own suffering? Is a great improvement in your marriage what you really want or deterioration to the point of permanent need for the concern of others? How vicious, yet subtle, is the demon of *self-pity.*

Perhaps you have always been afraid of people, of new situations, of the dark, of world war, of poverty, of going insane, of family disgrace, of rejection, of love, or of breaking with church tradition. On and on it goes. Or you may simply have a nameless anxiety which paralyzes you into indecision and inertia when wisdom calls for action or prompts you to flee when the only wise course is to stand your ground. The spirit of *fear* may have so crippled you that you do not even know what liberty in Christ is!

With some, the dictates of the flesh reign in supreme tyranny over life. Every decision is judged by whether it will gratify some carnal appetite. If your body tells you when you *must* eat, *must* drink, or *must* have sexual satisfaction, you may have lived under the dominion of the demon *lust.*

Do resentments swirl in your inner being after most of

your encounters with others? Is there an inner iciness which freezes other people out of your life, no matter how close they are supposed to be? Or does your hostility flame forth in a fire of vicious anger expressing itself with inflammatory words? You may be prey to the ruler demon *hate* binding you with invisible chains to a dungeon of loneliness and misunderstanding and making it impossible for you to love.

Once God put these words into my thoughts: *Startle every life you touch with the reality of my love.* Is it possible that His resources, not our own affections, are to be a fountain where the thirst of every human relationship is quenched? Could this fountain, fed from the underground stream in the wellsprings of the Father's love, ever run dry?

There is one more ruler spirit which has as its special characteristic the inability to submit to any other authority but itself. This wicked force has pervaded our age and swept the world's youth. Parading defiantly, it leaves in its wake anarchy which is erupting into violence, revolution, sexual depravity, drug abuse, or occultism. The spirit of *rebellion* captivates our youth and distorts their zeal for reform into craving for revolution. Satan has subtly provided the climate for this demon by powerfully undermining authority patterns across the globe. For a century this steady erosion has been taking place, but the last decade has seen it cascade into a landslide.

With Darwin's theory of evolution came the great modern challenge to the authority of the Bible as the Word of God. Concurrently many religious cults sprang up, most accepting some biblical truth but adding to and distorting it with further "revelation" of their own. Then came higher criticism, neo-orthodoxy, and theological liberalism, each distinguished by an attack on the Word of God as infallible and authoritative. Added to this was the philosophy of John Dewey, giving rise to progressive education and the cult of modern permissiveness. Finally, we observe the new morality and situation ethics, logical after-effects of the steady decline of regard for all authority. Today we find a carefully engineered and diabolically prepared climate over which the man of sin (the beast of Revelation Chapters 13–18) will appear to offer the only solution to a world reeling under its own anarchy.

The genius and deadly poison of the demon *rebellion* is that it infects the young with perpetual immaturity. Only those who have submitted to rule are fit to rule. The Lord Jesus Christ made it clear that He never acted independently, but always did the will of His Father in heaven. His submission to God the Father was the secret of His perfect authority over every situation He encountered, even when living within the confines and limitations of human flesh.

Perhaps most deadly of all the ruler demons, however, is the spirit of *unbelief*. If not banished from the life and replaced with faith, it can lead the mind into insanity and the soul into eternal damnation (Hebrews 3:7–13, 6:1–9; I Timothy 4:1).

To our amazement we have met many Christians tormented by unbelief; some are mental patients and potential suicides for this reason. The demon unbelief is probably responsible for the widespread heresy that the ministries of power died with the first century church. The only permanent deliverance from it comes by *willing to believe* (John 7:17) and saturating the mind with faith-building scriptures.

It is regrettable that there are not more men who trust God's power today. Precisely here lies the tragedy of the decimated gospel. Multitudes around the world have asked Jesus Christ for the gift of eternal life, understanding very little of what is included in the package. The majority never even search His Word honestly to find out.

When Christ died on the cross, He not only died for our sins, He gave Satan and the demon world their death blow, ending their dominion over all who would repent and believe Him to the extent of crowning Jesus as Lord over their lives. When Christ rose from the dead, He not only shared His resurrection life with every believer. He went through this experience "that through death He might render powerless him who had the power of death, that is, the devil" (Hebrews 2:14).

Even though "when He ascended on high, He led captive a host of captives, and He gave gifts to men" (Ephesians 4:8), the greatest phenomenon of our age is a multitude of believers in Him who stay in their captivity to evil powers, and who despise and shun the gifts of their heavenly Bridegroom. They are much like the miserly hermit who lives a lifetime of poverty in a filthy shack to rise from obscurity only in death, when a fortune is found hidden with his corpse.

One does not need to argue with Christians today to find out whether they are baptized in the Holy Spirit or not. One needs only to look for the evidence of power and a constantly expanding witness for Jesus. It was He who said, "You shall receive *power* when the Holy Spirit has come upon you; and you shall be My *witnesses* both in Jerusalem, and in all Judea and Samaria, and even to the remotest part of the earth" (Acts 1:8). Jesus allowed for no alternate possibility. He did not say we *may* get His dynamite, or we *may* be His witnesses in an ever-widening circle of influence which covers the globe. He said we *shall.* The only "if" clause is related to the coming of the Holy Spirit upon us.

It is worthwhile to note that many of the salvation verses of the New Testament use the Greek preposition *eis* meaning "into." The Holy Spirit must come into the believer at conversion, or we cannot be regenerated and given new life in Christ. However, the preposition *epi* meaning "upon" is the one used in Acts 1:8, and in every instance in the book of Acts where the Holy Spirit falls upon believers, this same concept is evidenced: The baptism in the Holy Spirit is a mantle of power and enduement for service to do what God wants done.

Just here we arrive at the root problem in many people today. They simply do not want to do what God wants done! They are not interested in casting out demons, praying in the Spirit with new tongues, picking up serpents, facing persecution so severe that only a miracle of God will bring them through it, or laying hands on the sick so that they will recover. Yet the Lord they profess to trust was the very one who said these signs would accompany those who believed. He has never changed His mind. Then as now "they went out and preached everywhere, while the Lord worked with them, and confirmed the word by the signs that followed."

The most tragic deception of our day is the work of Satan in stirring up the very people who claim to be champions of the Bible to fight bitterly against the work of the Holy Spirit. Spiritual cataracts blind their eyes as they read scripture dealing with the third person of the Godhead (His power and His gifts) and the many passages in the Word showing how Christ and His disciples dealt with Satan and demons. Such believers rationalize their position as biblical, saying that supernatural ministries are not necessary today, that they disappeared with the original apostles. Behind such an argument (which has no basis in Scripture), one can only suspect a demonic source. Thus it is futile to argue the point, for demons are irrational, their position irrevocable, and their final doom inevitable.

How will the conflict between their demonically inspired prejudices and the revealed will of God be solved? Perhaps the answer lies in an understanding of the great key of John 7:17. Jesus said, "If any man is *willing* to do His will, he shall know of the teaching, whether it is of God, or whether I speak from myself."

At the heart of all doctrinal heresy is rebellion against God's will; therefore the only way out of this wilderness is genuine repentance and humility before God. It would be good for one who earnestly loves Christ and wants the will of God in his life to get down on his face before Him alone and apart from every distracting influence.

Waiting on God with every pretense put aside, we can ask Him the hard, searching questions. Could it be that I have been wrong, all these years? Could it be that what I have thought to be sound teaching has been interwoven with a demonic thread of unbelief? Have I really obeyed Your Word, Lord, or have I siphoned off that part which will make me despicable in man's eyes? Have I lost the fear of displeasing you through the awful fear of man which Your Word says brings a snare? Am I really half as concerned about the purity of the faith as I am for my own reputation? Does the insignificant persecution I've faced when I've proclaimed Jesus as Savior so offend me that I am afraid to be reviled as You were? Is it more worthwhile to keep my image—and the satanic bondages in me and my family—or to throw caution to the winds and be ridiculed as a tongue-speaker, a demon-driver, and a faith-healer? Am I ready for the kind of honesty You really want in me and my family? Can I face up to flaws in family relationships which demonic deception have conveniently hidden? What will happen to me if I resist Your perfecting work, Lord, as You get rid of the spots and blemishes in all of us? Can I risk facing Your return without the oil of Your Spirit brilliantly radiating light to all I meet?

How the Christian answers these questions may well determine his own fate and that of his family during the deepening darkness at the end of this age. It also may determine how much joy he will experience at the return of Christ and the kind of welcome he can expect from his Lord.

21
Getting the Home in Order

"If it doesn't work at home, we have nothing to export." So says Derek Prince.

Our family has found out, through God's jungle camp, just how true that is. Yet often Christian families stay strangely myopic at this point. They imagine that the marital strife and rebellious teenagers just happened. Or worse, they rationalize, concluding their family has been the brunt of satanic attack because of their outspoken witness for Christ (which may be true) and that they are at the mercy of such nonsense and can do nothing about it (which is never true).

God's citadel for light in this dark world is the Christian home. Ephesians 5:22–6:4 reveals that every believing family is to be patterned after the heavenly family. The wife's submission and respect for her husband are to point to the church's relationship with Christ. The husband and father's sacrificial love and capable headship are to point to Jesus' atonement and care for His people.

The closer we get to the end of this age, the greater the

contrast should be between homes where Christ is Head and those where He is ignored. Since this is true it is no wonder that Satan has aimed much of his strongest artillery at our families. His goal is to say to the world around us, "See? It doesn't work. They have nothing to export." Once we become aware of this fact, there is only one response worthy of children of God. "It's *got* to work, even if we have to give up all of our fondest ambitions in the process and we die in the attempt to make it work." Either we *can* do all things through Christ who gives us the strength, or we may as well call God a liar and ourselves hypocrites.

Perhaps a brief review of the adversary's tactics for the past hundred years will shed light on our present-day family predicaments. While he was busy undercutting the authority of the Word of God with the rise of Darwinism, neo-orthodoxy, heretical cults, educational permissiveness, and moral laxity, Satan was declaring all-out warfare on the biblical roles of the sexes. With the first sculpturing of modern feminism, chips came away from the male role as authority in his home. The husband as the head who gave the wife her derived authority came to be replaced by an equal team, neither having the final say.

Along with this confusion, which provided our modern unisex phenomena, came a corresponding dilemma. How can women respect and submit to men that are less than men? How can men love, cherish, and reign over women who are less than women? In a majority of families today, this issue remains unresolved. Instead of a solution, unhappy inmates of marital prisons resign themselves to something known as "the battle of the sexes," the worst casualties of which are the unfortunate offspring. Sometimes it makes little difference whether retreat from the battle is sought in separation or divorce, or whether coexisting enemies decide to maintain the domestic cold war intact "for the sake of the children." The end result will still be *defeat*—unthinkable for the believer who is always to triumph in Christ.

Satan has done his work well. Our whole culture is reeling under the staggering impact of familial and moral anarchy

Emasculated men and defeminized women, imagining that they have only to deal with a humanized God, are a law unto themselves. In one short generation we have seen divorce and immorality rise to epidemic proportions, and homosexuality mushroom to a place where its champions are demanding legal rights.

Throughout these modern Dark Ages, the devil and his army have apparently been directing their primary efforts against the man's role as authority and decision-maker. Then they compound the problem by enlisting women to usurp that role. This cunning trick works today as successfully as it did in the Garden of Eden. In fact, one wonders whether the whole history of the human race would have been different if Eve had consulted her husband before yielding to the serpent's advice!

Since all earthly families are meant to be patterned after the heavenly one, any distortion of roles here makes it very difficult for the young to discover God as Father. What son yearns to grow up, get married, and have children, if he sees that family relationships are the source of Daddy's greatest misery? Who wants to be like an indecisive, vacillating, compromising nonentity? Does the passive father who abdicates his role deserve the reverential submission of his wife and children? Why emulate a perfunctory captain of a ship without helm or rudder, clearly headed for the rocks in stormy seas?

When a girl looks at her earthly father, does she see a model for the man she wants to give lifetime allegiance? Can she picture the heavenly Father and Bridegroom to whom she will give eternal allegiance? Where, in her mother, does she see those rare, feminine qualities that submit to and build up such a man?

Children love to imitate, but whom shall they mimic? Does the mother teach anarchy by her defiant attitude toward her husband? If she does, why is she surprised at the phenomenon of rebel sons and daughters? If she is a domineering shrew to whom her husband has long surrendered to keep peace, can she honestly wail at the tragedy of sons and daughters who reject the institution of marriage? Even though the new morality is nothing but the old immorality, is it any wonder that so many people choose it today in preference to lifetime imprisonment?

A friend has a daughter who became a hippie and lived with several young men in succession. Since one relationship seemed more enduring than others, the Christian mother asked the girl why they did not marry. "You've got to be kidding, Mom," came the answer. "You think I'd ever get stuck with anyone the way you are with Dad? Why, if I get treated the way you have, I'll just walk out, that's all."

A key to freedom from satanic oppression is getting the home into God's order. During this past year, the Lord has shown us that this is just as important as renouncing interest in the occult and forgiving everyone who has wronged us. Not only do we have the negative examples of Heidi and others who refused to set their houses in order, but we also have the positive proof of the glorious change in the Camerons and many others, as well as the change in our own marriage once we finally knuckled down to obedience.

I was late in learning. Handicapped by a marriage which had a rocky beginning, I held very little hope for a happy relationship. The best I could picture was stoic resignation toward our cataclysmic mixture of temperaments: a heroic front of forced cheerfulness with each other intended to fool our children. Of course I was the only one who was deceived. The children knew very well how things really stood.

One day Beth Ann started to cry at the supper table; then she ran out to the family room. I followed after her, unable to understand. I put my arms around her and held her close, begging her to tell me what was wrong.

"It's you and Daddy, Mommy," she whispered through her sobs in a moment of rare candor toward one whom she had come to think of as the big boss.

I was stunned. Shock waves pounded my consciousness with a whole set of new ideas. *If our failure in marriage is so evident that our children are being emotionally upset, we'd better do something about it,* I decided. What has happened in the interim is one of the greatest miracles we have seen. Once God finds that we are *willing* to do His will, things really begin to happen.

My biggest problem right away was *how* to change? We were obviously on the wrong tack, but how did we come about and get on the right one? Once I began to seek God in earnest about this, however, He began making the answers increasingly clear.

The first glimmer of light came through something I heard which shot at the heart of a huge deception of mine. For years I had assumed Dick and I had made the wrong marriage. What good could possibly come of a step like that? Then someone said, "It doesn't matter half as much who you marry as *who you are.*"

This statement has the ring of truth to it and was completely consistent with Scripture on the subject of God's grace. In fact a common explanation of that grace is that God doesn't work with what He finds; He works with what He brings.

In the fall of 1970 the Lord again used Don Basham to bring truth into my life. For four days Don ministered here in the Albany-Troy-Schenectady area and for one of them was a guest in our home. Here he had opportunity to observe the undercurrent of friction between Dick and me at close hand. He knew I was in the deliverance ministry myself, but I was finding it hard to get Dick to work with me. I complained to Don about that, and he answered me in a cryptic way.

"You'd better watch out, Pat, or you may end up having your head uncovered," he said.

Although I did not understand what he meant and had no opportunity at the time to ask him to explain it, I was really anxious to find out. My prayer for light about this was answered so quickly that I got the impression the Lord had been waiting to teach me this truth for a long, long time!

Just a few days after the special meetings, our pastor preached on 1 Corinthians 11:10, "Therefore the woman ought to have a symbol of authority on her head, because of the angels." He pointed out that the *New American Standard Bible* puts *a symbol* in italics, which means that it is not in the original text. Therefore the sense of the passage is really that a woman should be under authority in order to protect herself against the activity of fallen angels or demonic spirits. For a married woman this means she must submit to the headship of her husband.

Now I had known these scriptures for years, but I had never really understood them. Suddenly I saw that submission to Dick was not some kind of spiritual hors d'oeuvre; it was dire necessity—the bread and meat of a healthy, free Christian life. Once I had thought I might have to *leave* Dick to get through life in one piece. Now I determined to *stick* to him like Scotch tape—for the same reason!

God is not joking when He says the truth will make us free. As soon as I began to see the light on this subject, I tried to walk in it. Sometimes my toddling was unsteady, and often I fell and bruised my knees in the process. But the Lord held my hand through it all, and He has led us both into an exciting adventure as He has begun to make our marriage over into the blueprint He always had in mind.

While Don Basham had been ministering in our area, Dick received the baptism in the Holy Spirit and release in the prayer language. Thus I reasoned that Dick was now fully empowered to take the lead in all ministry sessions, and I told him so. I pointed out that I was frankly embarrassed, and had been for some time, ministering in front of him. Now that we had the Friday night prayer meetings when both of us were present, the situation had to be changed.

To my great joy, Dick agreed to take authority over the spirits and give the commands to cast them out. Our very first prayer meeting after Don left, Dick handled the group efficiently and has been doing so ever since.

For Christmas a dear friend gave me the book *Fascinating Womanhood,* by Helen Andeline. I have to admit that this was fairly strong medicine for a toddler, and there were days when I just had to put it down. Some things this woman said aroused real fury in me, and I began to be suspicious of the source of this strong reaction. One day while I was taking a shower, I asked God why I felt this way about that book. The word *rebellion* flashed through my mind.

"Why of course that's it!" I said right out loud. "I renounce you, you spirit of *rebellion*, in Jesus' name. You leave me at once."

Nothing happened while I was in the shower or getting dressed, but as soon as Dick walked in the door that night for supper, chaos reigned. To my amazement I found myself pounding the kitchen counter with my fists and yelling at him at the top of my lungs. There had been no incident, no real provocation for my outburst. I was ashamed and disgusted with myself when it was over, and I apologized to Dick and the whole family. Before long I realized the demon had left as it put on this little show characteristic of its name!

One night while we were getting ready for bed, I admitted to Dick that the trait of his which had bothered me the most over the years was his lack of forcefulness. I could hardly believe my own honesty as I told him I had always wanted some strong, masterful man to run my life, and I felt he had let me down.

Now it was Dick's turn to bang his fists down on the edge of the bed, but it was a real turning point for us. Once he knew I hated the role of leadership he had so often delegated to me (either through resentment or indifference), he no longer expected it of me!

That night I turned the check book over to him with all the bills. I have had no concern for any of those matters since. Now I just ask Dick whether we can afford something or not, and that is the end of the discussion. What he says goes—and the children know it.

Another change that had to come in our home was in the matter of child discipline. For years most punitive measures had come from me with the result that my image was a harsh one while Daddy was the easygoing "nice-guy." I had some fairly strong feelings about all this, and I told Dick so. Providentially my mother gave us our copy of *The Christian Family* by Larry Christensen (published by Bethany Fellowship), just as we were tackling this problem. This book is a master-piece of summary and analysis of biblical roles in the family. Christensen makes it clear that the father is to be the au-thority figure in the home; the one who metes out corporal punishment to the children and other forms of discipline to the young people. The mother is only responsible for their correction in the father's absence.

Now when one of our active tribe acts up, I simply look up to their father, perhaps with an expectant "well?" if he is slow to get the hint. He does the spanking and lays down the edicts *when he is here.* This change has done more to change our relationship with our children than any other shift of this past year. Mother is now no longer the ogre, schoolmarm figure in all situations.

Once I could relax more with them, I have begun to take time for the "fun things." It is exciting teaching Beth Ann to cook and helping our first grader, Billy, learn to read. Certainly our teenagers feel more comfortable in an envi-ronment where their father is having his say. Their respect for him and appreciation of him have improved as he has assumed more and more of the responsible, authoritative role in this home. Dick was always good about doing things with them; what was needed was an erasing of the pal image and substitution of the concerned and loving father image which is in harmony with Scripture.

Even with Dick taking the lead in spiritual ministry, family discipline, and finances however, we had a long way to go to make our own relationship smoother. After my deliver-ance from the spirit of *rebellion* and recognition of its influ-ence on our marriage, I still had other areas of satanic decep-tion to uncover. The main attitude needing change was a basic mistrust in Dick's *ability* to lead effectively since I had seen him fail to do it for so long.

Once I asked a close friend how to tackle this problem. She looked long and hard in my face, then announced, "Just let him fall on his face and *make* a mistake, if need be." God must have opened my mind, for it dawned on me that she was right. The top of any chain of command has no one to congratulate—or to blame—for his decisions. He must make them and accept the consequences.

Perhaps the most difficult moment of truth came for me, however, when I realized that I must emphasize my own weaknesses if I were ever to inspire in Dick the desire to take care of me and watch over me as the protector every woman wants. It was hard to know when to admit to physical tiredness or inability, for instance, or when to fight laziness. Oddly enough, God intervened here in a surprising way. My health became a problem again—a battle not over yet. I simply cannot sit up reading and typing until midnight or 1:00 A.M. and still get up at 6:30. Often I have to get to bed right after supper. Dick has been so understanding through all of this that I wonder how we ever survived through my ultra-independent years. Now he regards it as one of his prime duties to take care of me, even insisting that he do all the driving on a recent vacation trip to Maryland and back. This represents a real sacrifice on his part, for he does not enjoy distance driving, and we usually share this responsibility.

I am genuinely thankful for these things, and God has been showing me I must tell Dick so. How little we praise those in our own families, and what a difference it makes when we start to notice their many kindnesses! I had not realized how much criticism was going on in our home until all of us recently made a concerted effort to cut it out and start praising one another, with a system of fines for backsliders.

Reflecting now on our home, I can honestly say that during this past year God has taken it out of the minor key and put it into a major one with love and praise as the basic chord to which every interpersonal relationship is harmonized. We are not at all perfect and sometimes still have days when we have ill tempers or discord; but the great difference is that now we recognize such things as sour notes in the family harmony. Before, they seemed perfectly natural, because we worked together in such a discordant way. The switch from Shostakovich to Haydn has helped all of us. No wonder we find it easy to raise our hands and say, "Hallelujah, praise the Lord," in our own family devotions every night after supper.

Recently a friend who has resisted her husband in countless subtle ways came to see me. Listening to her talk for over two hours, I realized that her home was quite different from ours. The husband had never had difficulty assuming his authoritative role; his failure to follow the scriptural pattern of Ephesians 6 lay in the area of lack of love. He has ruled over his family as an absolute tyrant, picayune about the smallest details of compliance to his will. Yet he withholds affection from his wife and children, refuses to spend time just having fun together with them, and is stingy with them in financial matters. The result has been a tragic situation where the wife gets back at him in every way she can. Her lack of submission to him has not been taught to the teenagers, but it has been caught by them. These unhappy young people are true rebels, not only to their parents but also to the Lord. Rejection of the gospel has proved their most effective and heartbreaking weapon against the outrage they feel toward living in such an emotional climate.

When Linda was talked out, she asked me what I felt the solution was. I shared the light our pastor had given on 1 Corinthians 11:10 and told her how the Lord had worked in my own life through understanding this truth.

"So you see," I said in conclusion, "when you get down to the nitty-gritty, women have to face an inevitable truth. Either we submit to our husbands, or we may end up at the mercy of the demons. Which is worse, to be subject to your husband or subject to the demons?"

"Frankly, I can't see very much difference," Linda said, laughing bitterly.

"Oh no?" I went on. "Then maybe you and I should take a trip up to the State Hospital and find one of those back wards where there are schizophrenics sitting on the floor in their own urine who haven't said a word to anyone in two or three years. Then I'll ask you that question again."

The point had hit home. It was unnecessary to say anything more. Whether Linda will truly submit to her husband, however, is up to her. Only time will tell which choice she has made. One would hope that her husband could begin to show love in ways that are meaningful to her, by showing concern for some of the things she wants to do or allowing her some money to spend on herself and the children however she would like. One would like to think that he would cease to criticize her constantly and begin to praise her for small things instead. But here again, the choice is his. No one can live the lives of others for them.

Perhaps the greatest temptation Satan is plaguing Christian husbands and wives with these days is despair and a feeling that it is hopeless to try to change the status quo. We thank the Lord our own experience proves how wrong that is. God is a God of new beginnings. Anyone willing to do His will and change his role to fit the biblical pattern can begin to see improvement immediately.

Julie was one of the most unhappy wives I have ever met; yet since she and Roger have brought their home into God's order, she now has an amazing testimony. When I last saw her she told me she now wakes up every morning thanking God for giving Roger to her as her husband. Think of it, a marriage once beset by almost every kind of problem now looked on as the happiest fact of her life!

This is not sham; this is reality. And it proves in an eloquent way that the One who changed the water into wine is still transforming the dull, mundane, even ugly things of life into sparkling experiences of joy. Jesus was there at your wedding whether you invited Him or not. He's there in your home right now waiting for you to invite Him to take His rightful place as Head and to get in line, in order, behind Him.

Can you do a better job of running your home than He can?

22
An Unavoidable Choice

If there were ever a time when we could decide how much we'd take of God and then push back from the table with "That's enough, thank you," that time is gone for good. Lines are being clearly drawn for the struggle which will end this age, and we are either on the Lord's side or in the enemy camp. The Jesus people have it right when they point the finger heavenward signifying He is the *one way* to God.

A prominent charismatic conference speaker said a special meeting was recently called in Southern California of a department with some responsibility for the security of the United States. They were to investigate the strangest danger ever reported to this group of men. Sweeping into our country, across various points of its territorial borders, hordes of dark, shadowy figures have been observed on our radar screens. Soon after such an invasion, the area entered had erupted in chaos. Ghetto and campus violence, large concentrations of drug addicts and hippie pads, as well as corruption and excessive Mafia activity were noted in these areas.

Yet these dark invaders cannot be photographed or observed with the natural eyes. For this reason government officials are able to do nothing about such reports or in any way hold back future invasions. Indeed, the men called to study this problem were at a loss to know just what kind of problem it is or how the government can do the slightest thing about it.

Those of us who understand spiritual warfare realize the appeal has been made to the wrong government. The only effective stand which can be made against these foes is in the *kingdom of God.* The only group of individuals qualified to take a stand against these enemies is the body of Christ. Yet the members of this body are largely asleep, while the peril increases, and the clock makes its way irrevocably toward midnight.

What shall be done to right this situation? Those who belong to the Lord Jesus Christ face an unavoidable choice. Either we shall rise to our feet and stand against the unseen foes in the power of His might, or we shall be inundated by them.

It is alleged that nearly two centuries ago George Washington, a man of God, sought divine guidance before attempting the apparently suicidal crossing of the Delaware. After fasting and waiting on God for some time, the general was visited by an angel of the Lord who showed him in a vision the three great crises of America's destiny.

The first such crisis was the Revolution in which the colonies were engaged. Washington was encouraged to cross the Delaware and proceed to a victory assured to him by God.

The second crisis was shown a war in which brother would fight against brother. It was promised that though it would be severe, the republic would remain intact.

The third and greatest crisis was pictured as being initiated by huge hordes invading our land from foreign shores. In his vision the amazed general was shown great cities, non-existent in that time, going up in flames. Then the general saw the battered remnant left in the land, that had been lying on the ground as if soon to perish, rise to their feet and drive the enemies away. The source of their help was another army in the air above them, clothed in light, and engaged in conflict with the shadowy invaders!

Why was Washington shown these things except that God wanted His people to be prepared for this struggle and respond in His way?

We may be sure God did not provide this vision as a form of religious entertainment. He never wastes anything; He must have wanted this account preserved for those for whom it would be relevant. Could the strange invaders on the radar screen be those of Washington's prophetic vision?

Many of us believe that the wheels are now in motion which will bring this age to a close, and no human whim or effort will stop them. The essence of reality in our day is to find out what God is doing and get in on it.

His purposes now may be compared to a great river, thundering on its course and sweeping aside all debris as it plunges toward its goal. Occasionally an ancient rock, imbedded deep in the river bed, may be seen jutting its obstinate, stationary form above the current. Never mind, the river just passes it by.

Some of God's people are like that. They live in the river of God's life, but they refuse to move with Him with the inevitable result that the river rushes by them. They are bypassed and forgotten in the unalterable flow of God's mighty current. They never experience the adventure of riding the rapids with God. How are they to know the joy of coming into the huge gulf of His peace in union with the rest of His Spirit-led and anointed children from around the world?

It has been pointed out by prophetic speaker Hilton Sutton that most of the charismatic lay movements within the historical churches were started after the Six Day War of June 1967. Israel's miraculous victory took old Jerusalem out of the hands of the Gentiles and fulfilled Luke 21:24. No wonder God is on the move in the Gentile world. The times of the Gentiles are in the process of being fulfilled!

In some ways the severest scriptural warning to the church

concerning the end times is the parable of the ten virgins recorded in Matthew 25:1–13.

> Then the kingdom of heaven will be comparable to ten virgins, who took their lamps, and went out to meet the bridegroom. And five of them were foolish, and five were prudent. For when the foolish took their lamps, they took no oil with them, but the prudent took oil in flasks along with their lamps. Now while the bridegroom was delaying, they all got drowsy and began to sleep. But at midnight there was a shout, "Behold, the bridegroom! Come out to meet him." Then all those virgins arose, and trimmed their lamps. And the foolish said to the prudent, "Give us some of your oil, for our lamps are going out." But the prudent answered, saying, "No, there will not be enough for us and you too; go instead to the dealers and buy some for yourselves." And while they were going away to make the purchase, the bridegroom came, and those who were ready went in with him to the wedding feast; and the door was shut. And later the other virgins also came, saying, "Lord, Lord, open up for us." But he answered and said, "Truly I say to you, I do not know you." Be on the alert then, for you do not know the day nor the hour.

Considering the lateness of the hour, we must adjust not only our priorities but also our behavior patterns. The Bridegroom will soon be at the door, and only those with oil keeping their lamps brightly burning will be ready. Several questions seem to be raised by this imperative.

Have you ever met Jesus in a personal way? When He comes will He know you as one of His intimate friends?

He said, "This is eternal life, that they may know Thee the only true God, and Jesus Christ whom Thou hast sent." Any experience of Him short of knowing Him personally is also short of eternal life.

Yet, as Dr. G. Allen Fleece often said, "He only waits to be wanted." Right where you are you can tell Him you are fed up with life plagued by sin and failure and ask Him to come in and take over. You have His promise, "The one who comes to Me I will certainly not cast out."

Now whether you have just made that step as you read the

last paragraph, or whether you have known the Lord Jesus Christ for many years, you may realize you need *power* to lead the life He expects of you. Your wick is there, but the supply of oil is far too small to provide the kind of light needed in the darkness where you walk. You need to be baptized in the Holy Spirit.

The Lord Jesus Christ is moving in a sovereign way today, pouring out the oil of the Holy Spirit upon His people. All over the world He is showing Himself still to be the "one who baptizes in the Holy Spirit" (John 1:33) just as He is still the "Lamb of God who takes away the sin of the world" (John 1:29). Since Christ is the Baptizer, you need only to ask Him in faith for this mighty immersion into the power of God. However, He will fulfill His promise to you on His terms, not yours.

If you approach Him with some such nonsense as "Lord, I want the power, but I do not want to speak in tongues," you are wasting your time. It would be like a bride saying to her husband, "I want your checkbook, but I refuse to let you touch me." The power is a result of the deepest union possible with the Holy Spirit. Scientists tell us that the most complex portions of the human brain are those which control speech. When the Holy Spirit has been allowed to invade and direct here, He has truly been given lordship of our deepest selves. Then we see Christ's promise to us fulfilled: "He who believes on Me, as the Scripture said, 'From his innermost being shall flow rivers of living water.'"

Every day of our lives we meet situations or know of problems which defy solution even when attacked by our best human wisdom. Thus every day we have a need for the prayer ministry of the Holy Spirit through us. Paul could say, "I shall pray with the spirit and I shall pray with the mind also; I shall sing with the spirit and I shall sing with the mind also. I thank God, I speak in tongues more than you all" (I Corinthians 14:15,18). The final piece of armor which he mentions as essential for the believer fully clothed for the conflict with Satan is prayer *in the Spirit* (Ephesians 6:18). The great thrill of my own spiritual life was not in those first few minutes in March of 1970, speaking forth a few syllables in the prayer language which He gave to me. Frankly, that was somewhat disappointing. The great joy has come through the *daily* times of praying and singing in the Spirit which have liberated my heart to praise God in a way impossible to my human mind and have effected intercession for others which has brought startling answers to complex problems. God can do anything but fail! Therefore I assume He will work out a perfect solution for any situation He is allowed to handle in His way. Now life is an exciting adventure, and I can hardly wait to see what He will do in each new day.

Sometimes, however, a believer will not be able to receive the release in the Spirit even when he earnestly wants all God has for him. Usually the problem here is demonic and should be attacked as shown throughout this book. The occult sins and all others must be renounced and confessed, every human being must be forgiven, and there must be a firm resolve to get the family and all authority relationships into divine order. Then in the name of Jesus Christ, one is able to make the verbal attack against Satan, his key demon and all others hindering the work of the Holy Spirit, and get rid of them, usually one by one. You can do this for yourself or you can get help in a group of believers, but by all means "press on toward the goal for the prize of the upward call of God in Christ Jesus." Never stop short of all He has for you.

Once you are empowered by the Holy Spirit, you will notice that the entire battle of your life is now centered on the issue of *light.* God wants it to shine freely and brightly from the lamp of your daily life; the powers of darkness will do their best to hinder or obscure it. Knowing what is going on is a big help in knowing how to fight.

God has a plan for keeping the oil flowing freely into your lamp, but He expects you to cooperate with Him in carrying it out. In the Old Testament tabernacle, priests had to come to the laver (a basin with water in it) every day for cleansing. In the New Testament Jesus prayed, "Sanctify them in the truth; Thy Word is truth." He also told his disciples, "If you abide in My word, then you are truly disciples of Mine; and you shall know the truth, and the truth shall make you free." Spending time with God every day reading His Word will cleanse you and build godly character as nothing else can. It is in this way that the fruit of the Spirit is developed. Power to do the supernatural things God wants done comes with the baptism in the Holy Spirit, but fruit must be fed and watered in order to grow. This takes time and daily progress; there are no short cuts in producing it.

George Müller, a man of great faith in the nineteenth century, found that the secret to a victorious Christian life was to spend time with God every day before he dealt with any human being. He began his quiet time on his knees with his Bible open before him. After a simple prayer of thanks and praise to God and a request for guidance, he read the chapters for that day. Then he began to pray about what was suggested to him in the Word of God. He found that this kept his mind centered on those things which concern God, but he also found that the simplest requests of his from a right motive never went unheard! Müller's life is a stirring testimony to the faithfulness of God in answering prayer.

I decided to try this for myself too. It works! Studying the Word on your knees at the beginning of the day, followed by praise and prayer, will change the course of life and get it into the mainstream of adventure with God.

Müller's goal was for his own soul to be happy in Jesus before the day began. We would do well to follow his example. Some days we have to take more time to confess sins or forgive others as God shows us these sins. Other days will just be spent in loving the Lord and telling Him so. How long has it been since you told the heavenly Father that you loved Him?

God's plan for the free flow of the oil of His Spirit through your life includes praise. Kay Herring, an older missionary we met in Nigeria (now retired), has a radiance and joy about her that is infectious. In those days when I was under such severe demonic oppression myself, I was desperately seeking answers. Naturally I noticed Kay's noticeable victory and asked her about it.

She told me a surprising story. Once she had become very depressed and joyless in her service for the Lord. She told her problem to Malam Badam, a national who worked in the mission dispensary. He said, "Try praise." She did, and her life was transformed.

Recently I heard a perplexing sermon by a man of God for whom Dick and I have love and respect. He was trying to show his people that they must learn to praise God; after all, there is a great deal in the Scriptures about this subject. He said it might do believers good if they got out in the woods and just began saying, "Praise God, praise you, Jesus," even though they wouldn't do that in church.

At this point I had to hang on to the pews with both hands to keep from standing up and asking him, *Why not? What's church for anyway? Are we just playing games or do we really come to pray and worship God?*

Where pastors and people are seeing this light, dramatic changes are taking place in lives and communities. A year ago a group of us here in Saratoga County formed a New Testament Fellowship. We meet in a home, just as believers did in the early church. Our teaching elder is a Spirit-baptized former Baptist pastor. He came into the life in the Spirit some years ago, and God has taught him much in the past years. He has taught us to raise our hands and praise the Lord—right in church!

Another great joy we have is singing in the Spirit. Someone with an excellent voice begins singing "Hallelujah" or "Praise God" on some note, and we all join in, in unison or in harmony. Soon the living room, where the forty or fifty of us are packed in, is filled with glory. It is then that things begin to happen. We usually do not attempt any of the miraculous ministries until there has been a free flow of praise in our midst.

One Sunday morning Charlene Strott (Beverly's daughter, chapter 10) came up to our pastor at the end of the service. She announced that she did not want to wear glasses any more and was sure God would heal her eyes. Charlene had a serious visual defect, and the opthamologist had assured her parents that she could never be without her glasses, which had lenses like the bottoms of soda bottles. They also required frequent checkups and changes in prescription, which involved expensive trips to Philadelphia. Humanly speaking, the adults present that Sunday morning could have found many reasons to discourage Charlene's faith. Fortunately, God overruled instead.

After the pastor called the rest of the elders present, the men anointed Charlene with oil, laid hands on her, and prayed. Then they advised Charlene to take her glasses off in faith, provided her father would agree with this plan. (Chuck Strott was out of town at the time.)

When Chuck got home, he was somewhat taken aback at the strange request of his daughter's to remove her glasses. However he agreed finally, with the stipulation that the decison of the doctor after the next checkup (about three weeks off) be final.

When the specialist examined Charlene's eyes, he took much more time than usual and seemed to be repeating the process several times. Finally he said, "I just can't understand it. There has been remarkable improvement in Charlene's eyes. In fact, there is nothing wrong with them, and she does not need her glasses any more."

This is one miracle from dozens which have happened right here in our fellowship. Multiply these by the thousands of groups where Jesus Christ is Lord and is believed for these things, and you get some idea of how mighty the present outpouring of the Holy Spirit is all over the world.

Many of us believe that we have only seen the beginning of what the Lord Jesus intends to do before He comes back. Suppose out of every hundred readers of this book, just one takes its message completely to heart and responds by acting upon it. He will soon be so liberated in his own life and so fired with God's life that he will find the Holy Spirit using him in countless ways with everyone he meets.

Soon he will have a group with him, taking God at His

word and being liberated by His power. Then each of these will fan out in an ever-widening circle of influence like the effect caused by small pebbles thrown into a still lake. Before long these lives will take on all the characteristics of the empowered witnesses promised by the Lord in Acts 1:8.

Our concern here in this fellowship has already gone far beyond our Jerusalem, the community in which we live. We are touching our Samaria in outreach to the ghettoes of Albany, our Judea in teaching ministries and conferences throughout the whole Capitol district, and are beginning to have a world view which cannot rest while the uttermost parts of the earth still need to know about Jesus.

How can we rejoice in God in our fellowship and not care about these others He loves just as much? There is one characteristic that clearly marks a child of God as different from those around him: he has love for the other members of the family. Scripture says, "We know that we have passed out of death into life, because we love the brethren. He who does not love abides in death" (1 John 3:14).

As Paris Reidhead says, the baptism in the Holy Spirit was not given to believers so that they might play "charismatic parlor games." This man directs Development Assistance Services, affiliated with International Students, Inc. which links up technological know-how and western capital with believers in all parts of the world, providing them with industry and a way to make a living. He points out that in Scripture as soon as God filled a man with His Spirit, he got "right to the point of the problem."

So it must be with us.

"Surely He shall deliver thee from the snare of the fowler," but for what purpose? To get up and give testimonies in smug groups, behind closed doors for the rest of our lives, to berate those who have not seen the light about the need for deliverance and empowering, to engage in doctrinal discussions and futile arguments?

Never! The purpose of God in delivering *you* from the powers of darkness and empowering *you* with His Spirit is to send you back into the conflict—this time on the offensive instead of the defensive. Here, "a thousand may fall at your side, and ten thousand at your right hand, but it shall not approach you . . . No evil will befall you . . . You will tread upon the lion and the cobra, the young lion and the serpent you will trample down."

One day the heavens will roll back as a scroll and the Lord Jesus will come in all of His shimmering glory. It will be too late then to run for oil for the lamp.

Appendix

Effective Scripture Verses to Memorize in Fighting
Through to Victory

1. *General Verses for Spiritual Warfare*

   James 4:7
   Luke 10:19
   Revelation 12:11
   2 Corinthians 10:3–5
   Ephesians 6:10–18
   Proverbs 18:10
   Mark 16:17
   1 John 4:1–4

2. *Verses to Use Against the Ruler Demons*

   HATE

   1 John 3:14
   1 John 4:16b, 19–21

   Song of Solomon 2:4
   Luke 10:27
   Matthew 22:37–39

Proverbs 10:12
Colossians 3:12–14
2 Thessalonians 3:5
Philippians 2:1,2
Ephesians 3:16–19
1 Corinthians 13:4–8a
Galatians 5:22,23

SELF-PITY

Nehemiah 8:10 (NASB)
Psalm 33:1
Psalm 34:1–3
Psalm 50:23
Psalm 104:33,34
Philippians 4:11,13,19
1 Timothy 6:6
1 Thessalonians 5:18

PRIDE

Proverbs 16:18,19
Proverbs 6:16–17a
Proverbs 3:34
Proverbs 13:10
Proverbs 15:25
Proverbs 16:5
Proverbs 21:23,24
Proverbs 29:1,23
2 Timothy 3:1,2
Philippians 2:5–8
James 4:10
1 Peter 5:6

FEAR

Psalm 56:3
Psalm 46:1,2
Psalm 107:2

2 Timothy 1:7
Isaiah 44:2b,3
1 John 4:18
Hebrews 13:6
Joshua 1:9

FEAR OF MAN

Proverbs 29:25
Joshua 1:5
Joshua 10:8

REBELLION

Proverbs 17:11
1 Samuel 15:23
Jeremiah 28:16
Jeremiah 29:32
2 Timothy 3:1,2
Ephesians 5:21
Philippians 2:5–8
Philippians 2:14
1 Thessalonians 5:18
Romans 12:1,2
Romans 13:1,2

UNBELIEF

Mark 11:23,24
Luke 1:45
John 8:31,32
John 7:38
John 6:29
Acts 27:25
1 Peter 1:6,7
Hebrews 11:1
Galatians 2:20
Mark 16:17,18

LUST

2 Timothy 2:22	Hebrews 12:14
1 Corinthians 6:9,10	1 Peter 2:11
1 Corinthians 6:17–20	Isaiah 52:11
1 Corinthians 3:16,17	Hebrews 13:4
Ephesians 5:3	Matthew 5:27,28
Leviticus 19:2	Titus 1:15

3. *Passages to Study on Related Subjects*

Fasting: Isaiah 58; Matthew 6:16–18
Praise: 2 Chronicles 20; Psalms 134–150; Revelation 4–5
Scripture: Psalm 119; John 8:31,32; Deuteronomy 4:1,2; Revelation 22:18,19
The Blood of Christ: Exodus 12; Hebrews 9–10; Revelation 5:9,10; Revelation 12:11

Bibliography

Basham, Don. *Can a Christian Have a Demon?* 1971; *Face Up With a Miracle,* 1967; *Handbook of Holy Spirit Baptism,* 1971; *Handbook of Tongues, Interpretation, and Prophecy,* 1971. Monroeville, Pennsylvania: Whitaker Books.

** *Deliver Us From Evil.* Washington Depot, Connecticut: Chosen Books, 1972.

Brooks, Pat. *Climb Mount Moriah.* To be published by Whitaker Books, Monroeville, Pennsylvania, 1973.

Brooks, Pat. *Occult Experimentation* (tract). Chicago: Moody Press, 1972.

——. *Using Our Spiritual Authority.* Monroeville, Pennsylvania: Whitaker Books, 1972.

Christensen, Larry. *The Christian Family.* Minneapolis: Bethany Fellowship, 1970.

Freeman, Dr. Hobart E. *Angels of Light.* Plainfield, New Jersey: Logos International Publishing Co., 1969.

Hagin, Kenneth. *Ministering to the Oppressed, The Authority of the Be-*

** This book has a directory of prayer meetings in its appendix, listing groups where deliverance meetings are a regular part of the ministry of these fellowships.

liever (pamphlets). Tulsa, Oklahoma: P.O. Box 50126, N.D.

Koch, Dr. Kurt. *Between Christ and Satan.* Grand Rapids, Michigan: Kregel Publishing Co., 1962.

Manuel, Frances D. *Though An Host Should Encamp.* Fort Washington, Pennsylvania: Christian Literature Crusade, 1971.

Penn-Lewis, Jessie, and Roberts, Evan. *War on the Saints.* Fort Washington, Pennsylvania: Christian Literature Crusade, N.D.

Peterson, Robert. *Are Demons for Real?* Chicago: Moody Press, 1972.

Whyte, Rev. H.A.M. *The Power of the Blood,* 1972; *Dominion over Demons,* 1969; *Pulling Down Strongholds,* 1971; *Hidden Spirits,* 1970; *Return to the Pattern,* 1966; *Fear Destroys,* 1968 (booklets). Scarborough, Ontario: 2 Delbert Drive.